HOOKED ON DRAWING!

ILLUSTRATED LESSONS & EXERCISES
FOR GRADES 4 AND UP

Sandy Brooke

PRENTICE HALL
Paramus, New Jersey 07652

Cover illustration by Lindsay Bolerjack

Library of Congress Cataloging-in-Publication Data

Brooke, Sandy.
    Hooked on drawing : illustrated lessons and exercises for
grades 4 and up / Sandy Brooke.
        p.   cm.
    ISBN 0-13-231853-9 (pbk.)
    1. Drawing—Study and teaching (Elementary)   2. Drawing—
Study and teaching (Secondary)   I. Title.
NC630.B76   1996
741.2'071—dc20

96-12022
CIP

Printed in the United States of America

    4 5 6 7 8 9 079 02 01 00 99 98

ISBN 0-13-231853-9

PRENTICE HALL
Paramus, NJ 07652

A Simon & Schuster Company

On the World Wide Web at http://www.phdirect.com

Prentice-Hall International (UK) Limited, *London*
Prentice-Hall of Australia Pty. Limited, *Sydney*
Prentice-Hall Canada Inc., *Toronto*
Prentice-Hall Hispanoamericana, S.A., *Mexico*
Prentice-Hall of India Private Limited, *New Delhi*
Prentice-Hall of Japan, Inc., *Tokyo*
Simon & Schuster Asia Pte. Ltd., *Singapore*
Editora Prentice-Hall do Brasil, Ltda., *Rio de Janeiro*

Acknowledgements

We wish to thank the following for permitting us to use their artwork:

The Art Institute of Chicago, Chicago, IL

George Wesley Bellows, *Elsie Speicher, Emma Bellows, and Marjorie Henri*; Alexander Calder, *Composition*; Claes Oldenburg, *Cube Tap (Plug)*; Ernst Ludwig Kirchner, *Head of a Young Man*; Gino Severini, *Train Crossing a Street*; Alberto Giacometti, *Portrait of the Artist's Wife Annette*; Willem de Kooning, *Untitled*; Frank Helmuth Auerbach, *Untitled (E.O.W. Nude)*; Jiri Balcar, *Four Figures at a Table*; Vincent van Gogh, *Landscape with Pollard Willows*; Pierre Bonnard, *Rooster*; Ben Shahn, *Monroe Wheeler*; Christo Vladimirov Javacheff, *Running Fence, Sonoma and Marin Counties, California*; Giorgio de Chirico, *Piazza*; Edgar Degas, *Dancer Bending Forward*; Constantin Brancusi, *The Studio*; Jean Debuffet, *Memoration XII*; Romare Bearden, *The Return of Odysseus (Homage to Pintoricchio and Benin)*; Johannes Bosboom, *Church Interior*; Shusaku Arakawa, *Separated Continuums*; Jack Beal, *Sleeping Bag and Pillow*; Joseph Goto, *Untitled (Single Figure)*; Jean Debuffet, *Untitled*; Arshile Gorky, *Three Forms*; Vincent van Gogh, *Corner of a Park at Arles (Tree in a Meadow)*; Jack Beal, *Fat Landscape*; Laurie Anderson, *New York Times, Horizontal/China Times, Vertical*; Georges Braque, *Collage*; Julio Gonzalez, *Screaming Head*; Paul Cezanne, *Sketchbook: Self-Portrait and Portrait of the Artist's Son, Chappuis 615*; Pierre Bonnard, *Lady with Curly Hair*; Max Beckmann, *Self-Portrait*; Claude Monet, *Caricature of a Man with a Large Nose*; Max Beckmann, *The Bathers*; Mary Cassatt, *Corner of the Sofa, Breeskin 14*

Muscarelle Museum of Art, College of William and Mary, Williamsburg, VA

Marino Marini, *Horse and Rider*; Abraham Walkowitz, *Six Figures*; Kathe Köllwitz, *Sorrowful Woman*; Paul Colin, *Figure of a Woman*; Marco Ricci, *Caricatures of Bandits*

San Francisco Museum of Modern Art, San Francisco, CA

Giacomo Balla, *Motivo con la parola buon Appetito*; Pablo Picasso, *Bust of Man*; Giorgio Morandi, *Vase with Flowers*; William T. Wiley, *It Probably Got in Through the Window*; Richard Diebenkorn, *Untitled*; Henry Moore, *Woman in Shelter in Winter*; Richard Diebenkorn *#10 from 41 etchings*; Robert Bechtle, *Nancy Reading*; Edward Ruscha, *Trademark 2*; George Braque, *Violin et compotier, (Violin and Candlestick)*; William T. Wiley, *Portrait of Apollinaire (Ooga)*; Richard Diebenkorn, *Seated Figure* from the portfolio *Ten West Coast Artists*

Stenbaum Krauss Gallery, New York, NY

Beverly Buchanan, *Waterfront Shacks*; Beverly Buchanan, *Blue Lightning*

The Hispanic Society of America, New York, NY

Francisco Jose de Goya y Lucientes, *Regozyo (Mirth)*

The Museum of Modern Art, New York, NY

Alberto Giacometti, *The Artist's Mother*

Minnesota Museum of Art, Saint Paul, MN

Simon Dinnerstein, *Marie Bilderi*

The Baltimore Museum of Art, Baltimore, MD

Larry Rivers, *The Last Civil War Veteran*

Collection of Lawrence and Ellen Benz, Bronxville, NY

Simon Dinnerstein, Red Pears

Glencoe Elementary School Teachers: Carol Davis, Linda Roberts, Alice McNassar, and Julie Winder

Harding Elementary Teachers: Patricia Pearson, Dennis Frates, Gary Hilberg, Bradd Jones, Gayle Larsen, Jepson Lonnquist, Jerry Borgens, and Claraine Ramadan

Corvallis Art Center: Lisa Platt and Hester Coucke

Prineville Middle School, Norm Borgaard

We wish to acknowledge the Artists Rights Society (ARS) for permission to reproduce the following:

© 1996 Artists Rights Society, New York/ADAGP/SPADEM, Paris
    Page 253 : Pierre Bonnard, *Lady with Curly Hair*.
    Page 102 : Pierre Bonnard, *Rooster*.
    Page 166 : Francis Picabia, *Entrance to New York*.

© 1996 Artists Rights Society, New York/ADAGP, Paris
    Page 157 : Constantin Brancusi, *The Studio*.
    Page 231 : Georges Braque, *Collage*.
    Page 183 : Jean Dubuffet, *Memoration XII*.
    Page 213 : Jean Dubuffet, *Untitled* (1966).
    Page 40   : Alberto Giacometti, *Portrait of the Artist's Wife Annette*.
    Page 248 : Julio Gonzalez, *Screaming Head*.
    Page 35   : Gino Severini, *Train Crossing a Street*.

© 1996 Artists Rights Society, New York/VG Bild-Kunst, Bonn
    Page 269 : Max Beckmann, *The Bathers*.
    Page 258 : Max Beckmann, *Self-Portrait* (1917).

© 1996 Willem de Kooning Revocable Trust/Artists Rights Society, New York
    Page 44   : Willem de Kooning, *Untitled* (1950)

Dedication

I have been very fortunate to have two parents who although they may have not always agreed with me, they have always supported me in my endeavors, sometimes happily sometimes unhappily. I owe them a great deal. This book is dedicated to

Alberta M. Griffith and Milton J. Griffith, my parents and my friends.

About the Author

Sandy Brooke has a Master of Fine Arts in painting and a Bachelor of Fine Arts in painting and drawing from the University of Oregon. She has taught painting and drawing for 20 years. It is through her experiences with students in grades K through 12 that she developed the projects and exercises for this book. The 17 years she spent working with students in the Artist-in-Education program were particularly formative. She worked with students all over the state of Oregon, not only teaching painting and drawing, but also developing large mural projects. In addition to teaching at the K-12 levels, she has been an instructor at Central Oregon Community College, Oregon State University, and the University of Oregon.

She has been a studio artist for 27 years and shows regularly in Oregon and the Western states. Her paintings are abstract, referencing real space and real people.

Anna Benedict, Grade 4, Ink and Wax Drawing

Introduction

Mankind's most enduring achievement is art. At its best, it reveals the nobility that coexists in human nature along with flaws and evils, and the beauty and truth it can perceive. Whether in music or architecture, literature, painting or sculpture, art opens our eyes and ears and feelings to something beyond ourselves, something we cannot experience without the artist's vision and the genius of his craft.

—Barbara Tuchman, Pulitzer Prize-winning historian[1]

I have worked in Oregon's Artist-in-Education program teaching painting and drawing to students in grades K–12 for 17 years. Over the years, the elementary teachers with whom I have worked have asked me if there was a book they could use that would guide them step by step through an art lesson, a book that would guide them through the fundamentals of the visual arts. Since I didn't know of one, I have designed this book for their needs.

Hooked on Drawing! comprises the lessons and exercises that have worked most effectively for me with students. It consists of exercises in which the students work through the formal art process—developing an understanding of the formal elements such as line, value or tone, texture, space, and perspective. There are no drawing or coloring assignments that involve preprinted forms. I have tried to design exercises that use and depend on the critical thinking process and that will develop decision-making skills. Each student must evaluate and interpret the guidelines presented in each exercise, then translate this information into a drawing. The drawings resulting from these exercises will be diverse and will represent each student's individual imagination and interpretation.

The exercises are designed for grades 4 and up. I have done some of these exercises with third graders who often, depending on their maturity level, have done quite well with them. Before the rules and the structure of art are taught, students should be encouraged to develop their imaginations by making the drawings and paintings stored in their imaginations. I have often heard from younger students at the end of a lesson, the request, "Can we draw what we want now?" They have ideas and they don't care how you properly shade a form or draw a house in perspective; they just like to draw. By the fourth grade, however, they have decided they want help and they want to know how to approach drawing. Their levels of perception and their skill level are greater than in the third grade. With these tools it is easier for them to take instruction. Each teacher should decide if students are ready to try a lesson, and even alter it to fit the students. Don't make an art lesson frustrating and complicated. If after you give the instructions they aren't quite following them, don't stop them; let them finish, and just do the same lesson again in a week. They will probably improve and hear more of the instruction. They don't have to follow the instructions to the letter. Let the guidelines be a framework to be filled in by the students. They will learn from their experience in trying to make a drawing.

Bonnie Pearce, Grade 4, One-Point Perspective

One of the advantages of an art lesson is that it reverses the thinking process other subjects depend on and develop, in which the teacher usually has the answer and the students work to figure it out. In art, the teacher presents the question and the students invent the answers. Every student may have a different answer within the parameters of the problem, and all solutions are acceptable. The visual arts offer each student the opportunity to be successful. This feeling of success is often a key to keeping students involved in school, and this success in art can translate to success in other subjects.

In the words of a brochure recently published by the South Carolina Arts Commission, "Through the arts perception is fine-tuned; thinking and feeling are necessary to proceed. In the arts students develop a sense of themselves. Art education develops self-esteem helping students succeed in life."[2]

A good example of this involves the exercise "Illustrating Science Words." This lesson was developed by a science teacher, Norm Borgaard, in Prineville, Oregon, who found his students had difficulty grasping the concepts of his space unit. He gave them a list of words including *thrust, gyroscope, rocket, booster,* and *Milky Way,* and asked them to draw what those words meant. In the end, the students understood, through visualizing the words, what they were studying in science. He also discovered that one of his students who was failing improved in all of his other classes as he began to have success in art. This success story is repeated again and again in the case studies that comprise the Getty Report, *Beyond Creating: The Place for Art in America's Schools,* published in 1985. The Getty report stated, "Art is fundamental to a child's learning, and is basic to education."[3]

The ultimate goal of an art lesson is to develop essential life skills. The South Carolina Arts Commission brochure on the advantages of having Art in the core curriculum concludes, "Students who study art learn to solve problems and make decisions; they develop informed perceptions; they participate well as team members; they can work with diversity; they learn how to organize, evaluate and interpret information. They become adept at making decisions concerning materials and techniques, and they learn to analyze specific tasks. The arts incorporate the basic skills of reading, writing, listening and speaking. All the qualities that lie at the heart of job performance."[4]

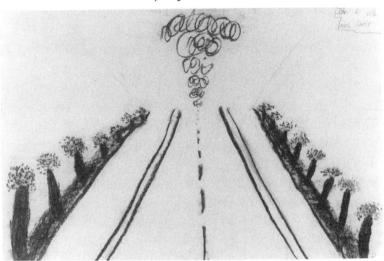

John Raglione, Grade 4, One-point Perspective, Charcoal

The importance of art has not been overlooked by the federal government. It is significant that Art has been designated one of the core curriculum subjects in President Clinton's Educate America 2000 plan, which is intended to rewrite America's current educational system. Art now stands shoulder to shoulder with Math, Science, Geography, Foreign Language, English, and History as an important part of our K–12 education.

The exercises in this book were designed to be simple and easy to use by teachers who range from those who know nothing of art to teachers who have strong backgrounds. *Hooked on Drawing!* is written so that a teacher who wants to have an art lesson at one in the afternoon can read about it in 15 to 20 minutes over morning coffee, assemble the supplies in 5 minutes, and present the art lesson comfortably and with assurance. Teachers have very full days and little time to prepare, especially for something new or outside their expertise. Each exercise is designed to be done in 30 to 45 minutes and is easily continued on the next day if necessary. From the first exercise to the last, many of the rules, processes, and guidelines remain the same. What at first may seem awkward will feel like "old hat" as you continue through the book. Never worry that you have done something wrong or that you have forgotten an instruction. You have just invented a lesson variation, and the students will produce a drawing from which they will learn more about the process. The elements of chance and surprise are the hidden components of the art process. Try these lessons yourself, along with your students. I've found students are very proud of their teacher's art work, and you will be more sympathetic to their distress in trying to do an exercise if you are trying to do it yourself. There are frustrations and pitfalls in these exercises that you can understand only by doing them.

There is not a "must do" order to the book, but by doing the foundation exercises, the warm-ups and practices first, you can create a base of knowledge on which to build and the more complicated lessons will be not only easier but more extensive in their scope.

Every student can learn to draw and every student has some talent if he or she is interested in art and doing art. In the beginning the students are often self-conscious about the quality of their drawings, but that's to be expected; learning to draw is like learning to walk. When we were born we couldn't walk but walking is a breeze now, and running is second nature. How is it they walk so easily now—the answer is of course, practice! Drawing is a learned skill, and it improves with practice.

Everyone can benefit from an art experience. Art is an individual experience and there is room for various and diverse forms of expression. This is evident when you look at the artwork I have selected to illustrate *Hooked on Drawing!* The artwork is from both students and professional artists. There are drawings from the most awkward to the most accomplished, and all are good. Look at the difference between the drawings of Jean Dubuffet and Edgar Degas or of Mary Cassatt and Willem de Kooning—all very famous and well-respected artists with completely different styles.

An art experience offers the students an opportunity for personal expression. Through the imagination, we develop our creative nature—our thinking and visualizing skills. The educational rewards of including the visual arts in the curriculum are endless, but more important, the arts can have a lifelong impact on students because they teach the foundation for what they hear, see, and perceive in the world around them.

Elliot Eisner, Professor of Education and Art at Stanford University, and author of numerous books and articles on art education summed up the value of the arts in education when he wrote, "The arts represent man's best work. Our children ought to have access to the intellectual and artistic capital of our culture."[5]

[1] Quoted in *Beyond Creating: The Place for Art in America's Schools,* a Report by the Getty Center for Education in the Arts, April 1985, p.20.
[2] South Carolina Arts Commission, Public Awareness Campaign, 1993.
[3] The Getty Report
[4] South Carolina Arts Commission
[5] The Getty Report

Neil Jansen, Grade 5, Ink, Wash and Wax Still Life

Mary Cassatt, American, 1844–1926, *Corner of the Sofa*, Breeskin 14, pencil study for the soft ground etching, c. 1897, 28.8 x 2 cm. Gift of Tiffany and Margaret Blake, 1967.145. Courtesy of the Art Institute of Chicago.

A PERSONAL NOTE TO THE TEACHER

The reason these exercises have been very successful with young students is not because they are in any way unique; it is because of the way in which they are presented. No student receives more praise from me than another. All solutions are acceptable. As long as the students are working and not fooling around all processes are acceptable. All work is hung up. All questions are important and treated as intelligent. Laughter is good. Talking to each other about the project is beneficial. Sharing skills is very good. Complimenting each other's work is better than criticizing each other. A teacher's praise should be specific and qualified so the students don't feel, "You're just saying that; you say that to everyone." A compliment should not be a general remark; try to refer to the character of the work—"Excellent line," or "Strong drawing!" Point out the strengths of the drawing.

I try to treat students as equals, in terms of all of us being involved equally in the art process. I respect their insights and questions and I have learned a lot from them.

These exercises are based on the fundamentals of drawing. I have presented many of the same lessons to my college classes. There is of course a different conceptual level and expectation for the college students but the actual exercise is the same. My experience has been that the students rise to the level of the teacher's expectation. They like learning to do art as artists do art.

Sarah Dubrasich, Grade 5, Continuous Line Drawing

GENERAL RULES AND GUIDELINES

1. Make sure the students do not draw on the back of the paper.

Art materials are like carbon paper. Marks made on the back of the paper will transfer to any surface that the art is hung on or set upon. Also, if both drawings are good, then you miss out on one. Student paper is often thin, which can result in bleeding through and ruining the drawing on the other side.

2. The students should not start over, rip up, or turn the paper over after starting a drawing.

Lines made "in error," or what the students think is in error, are actually helpful because now they know where they *do not* want the line to be, so they can move the line to the left or right, up or down. The rule of thumb is to start with light marks and then darken the final lines. The early lines will then be unnoticeable.

3. Ask the students not to cross out a drawing with an "X" or a scribble.

Each drawing experience teaches the student something. Drawing is not about perfect renderings. It's about learning to use the medium and learning to see things more completely and in depth.

4. Tell the students not to erase.

Erasing is reserved for the *end* of the drawing and should not be used during the drawing. Erasing is often used to clean finger prints off the surface. I will mention in the lessons where erasing is needed and when to use it.

5. The students should keep their drawing arms free.

Students should not lean on their drawing arms. A drawing starts in the eyes, with the brain processing and censoring information on shape, size, light, and color. That information is sent down the arm to the hand, which needs to react and move. If the hand, wrist, and elbow are flat on the desk, the student can react only minimally. If the student is standing up or kneeling on the chair, with the drawing arm dangling free from the shoulder, the lines and shapes flow more freely from the brain, through the arm, to the drawing hand. Students may support themselves with their nondrawing arms. They may rest the fingers and the side of the hand on the paper, but never rest the hand all the way to the wrist. Small desktop easels are helpful here.

6. Display student art.

An art show is a rewarding experience. Display student work as often as you can. The work can be mounted on construction paper or matted. I find the parents really like to see the work when they come to school.

7. Paper guidelines.

The lessons in this book will often use two or three sheets of paper per student. Give the students a new piece of paper when they have completed the exercise. This way students who work quickly can continue to work instead of sitting idly or bothering others. Another consideration for using additional sheets of paper is the composition of the space: While some students draw small enough to fit all of the objects on the paper, others may get only three objects on the paper before it's full.

8. Cultivate individual difference.

None of the guidelines or assigned processes of any lesson should be considered "carved in stone." Some students will miss an instruction, while some will try to do exactly what was assigned. This is not something to worry about or criticize the students for doing. It is better to accept unconditionally whatever the students produce.

Ben Verhoeven, Grade 6, Reversed Charcoal Drawing

TABLE OF CONTENTS

SECTION ONE: LINE DRAWING 1

Ben Verhoeven, Grade 6

SECTION TWO: VALUE AND MODELING 52

SECTION THREE: PERSPECTIVE 105

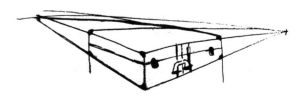

Amanda Chiavini, Grade 5

SECTION FOUR:
SPACE/SHAPE/PLANE 167

Blake
Shaw-Phillips,
Grade 5,
Chiaroscuro
Study,
Charcoal

SECTION FIVE:
TEXTURE 209

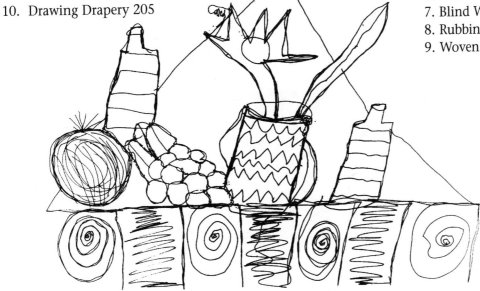

Caleb Ruecker, Grade 4,
Continuous Line Drawing, Ink

SECTION SIX:
PORTRAIT/PASTEL 244

SECTION SEVEN:
APPENDIXES 281

Sandy Brooke, American 1947, *Palmyra*, 1993. Charcoal on gessoed BFK, 30" x 40". Courtesy of the artist.

SECTION ONE
Line Drawing

Lindsey Dunn, Pencil Drawing, Tree, Grade 5

WARM-UP FOR PENCIL DRAWINGS
Foundation Exercise

BRIEF OVERVIEW

In an exercise class, students would start by stretching out and warming up the muscle groups. They should do the same before starting to draw. A warm up allows the students to experiment with their tools. Each tool is different, and each tool has particular qualities that should be tested before actually drawing with them. This can be a no-stress, playful time, and a time when students will discover things about drawing through making aimless marks and lines.

Pencils come in grades of lead. The B pencils get softer as the numbers get larger. The scale goes 2B, 3B, 4B, 5B, and 6B. The 6B is a very black and soft lead. This is the side of the scale artists use. On the other side are the hard leads more suitable for drafting and architects. The hard leads start at H and get lighter as they move to 2H, 3H, and finally to 6H, which is a very light lead and very hard.

Nathan Graff, Line Practice, Grade 3

THE EXERCISE

STEP 1: Holding the Pencil

There are two ways to hold the pencil in drawing. The first way is similar to holding a pencil to write an essay. Have the students hold the pencil as if they were going to write and then flatten the index finger down on the pencil as much as they can. Practice rolling the pencil between the forefinger and the thumb. Ask the students to try not to crunch the fingers back into the writing position but to relax the hand into the new position.

The second position (hand position 2) looks as if the hand is gripping the pencil under the fingers in the palm. Have the students take the pencil and lay it across the open palm, aiming the lead at the thumb. Next they gradually close the hand around the pencil until the thumb and index finger are comfortably holding the lead end between them. The thumb can now push and pull the pencil around the paper. The wrist is up and free.

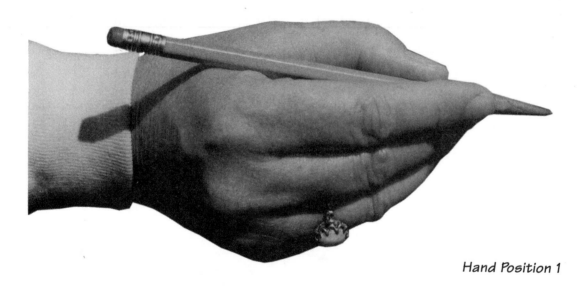

Hand Position 1

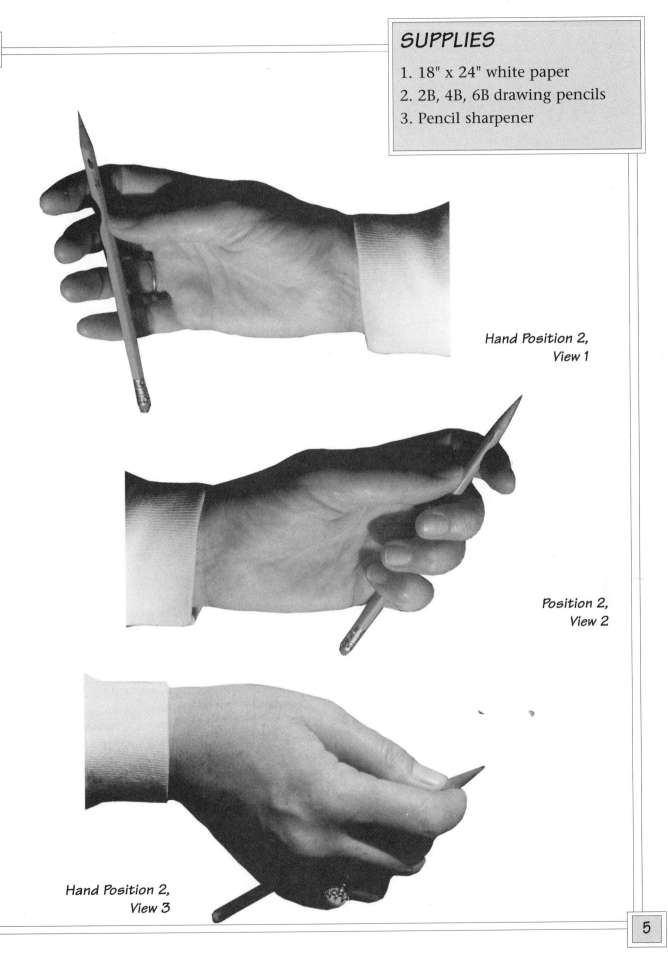

1. 18" x 24" white paper
2. 2B, 4B, 6B drawing pencils
3. Pencil sharpener

Hand Position 2,
View 1

Position 2,
View 2

Hand Position 2,
View 3

STEP 2: Making Light and Dark Lines with the Tip of the Pencil

Have the students start by using the tip of the pencil. (The pressure on the lead goes from light to firm.) Start with the 2B pencil and draw a line across the full 18 inches of the page. For the first three lines they should exert very little pressure on the pencil. Have them follow those first lines with a few more lines, increasing the pressure, then make a final four lines firmly pressing on the pencil. Don't press so hard that it breaks the lead. Using the 4B and 6B pencils, repeat the above rows of lines across the paper. The lines can be very close together.

Sarah Freilich, Grade 3, Line Weights

STEP 3: Using the Side of the Pencil Lead

The pencil lead has a tip and a side. This time, using Position #2 to hold the pencil, draw with the side of the lead. Start lightly and gently with the pencil on the side. Draw lines across the

entire 18 inches of the paper. Every few lines, gradually increase the pressure. The last lines will have worn the lead to a flattened state where the students can make very large and black lines. Press firmly but not hard. Hard pressure will break the lead.

Ben Verhoeven, Grade 6, Lines

Ben Verhoeven, Grade 6, Lines

STEP 4: Making Thick and Thin Continuous Lines

Have the students hold the pencil in position 2, then start a line with the tip of the pencil and without lifting the lead rotate the pencil over on its side. Then try to make a line that looks like a wave. Draw up one side on the tip of the pencil and draw down the other on the side of the pencil. Next try a series of big circle shapes. Draw one side of the loop with the tip and the other with the side of the pencil lead. Continue across the page with the big loops. The tip should make a thin line, the side should make a thick line.

Nathan Graff, Grade 3, Light to Dark Lines

STEP 5: Light to Dark Lines

Using all three pencils one at a time, draw a line that starts light, then by adding pressure, turns dark. Go all the way across the paper, changing the line from light to dark. This line is made with the tip of the pencil. Keeping the pencil in contact with the paper, press down firmly on the pencil, then let up, drawing as lightly as possible making one line. The students may draw curved or straight lines. Four Lines with each of the B, 3B, and 6B would be sufficient.

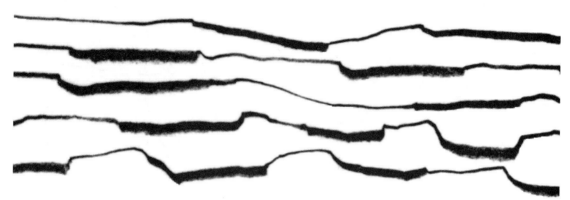

Ben Verhoeven, Grade 6, Thick and Thin Lines

STEP 6: Mark Making

Ask the students to use both the positions for holding the pencil, and to make as many different kinds of marks as they can think of (dots, dashes, spirals—make the marks light and dark).

Austin Shaw-Phillips, Grade 5, Mark Making

STEP 7: Gradation

Using the second position for holding the pencil, the students start *very lightly*, using the side of the pencil. Moving it slowly back and forth in a one inch area, they create a very light square of value. Ask them to continue the motion of the pencil moving up the page while increasing the pressure every inch or so. The width of the movement may also increase. They make wider and wider strokes as they make them darker and darker. This often looks like a tornado on their papers. This is the beginning of controlling value for use in shading. Ben's drawing here is a good example.

GOALS

This exercise is designed to develop hand-eye coordination, to familiarize the students with the possibilities of the pencil, to encourage learning by doing, and to encourage experimenting.

DISCUSSION/CRITIQUE

Put the drawings up and ask the students to discuss the marks. Do the marks remind them of anything? If so, what? Which lines could be used to make grass, mountains, oceans, birds, or clouds? In making a drawing, the type of line used may often define the subject. For example, all textures, hair and fur, or surfaces of leaves and tree trunks are described by combinations of marks, not by outlines.

Ben Verhoeven,
Grade 6,
Charcoal Gradation

SUMMARY STEPS

1. Practice using two positions to hold the pencil.
2. Change the pressure on the pencil.
3. Use the tip and side of the pencil.
4. Draw thick and thin continuous lines.
5. Draw light to dark lines.
6. Invent marks.
7. Practice shading by gradation.

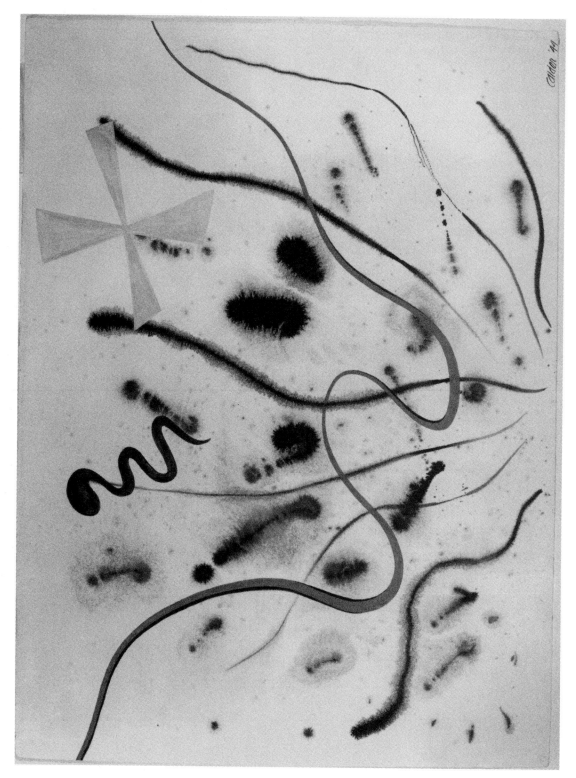

Alexander Calder, American 1898–1976, composition, gouache and watercolor on ivory watercolor paper, 1944, 57.1 x 79 cm. Gift of Mr. and Mrs. Thomas Rosenberg, 1957.96. Courtesy of The Art Institute of Chicago. All rights reserved.

DRAWING FROM A BAG I

BRIEF OVERVIEW

Learning to draw takes practice. Every mark is important, therefore nothing should be crossed off or X'd out. If a drawing isn't what the students wanted, have them draw the same object again on the same piece of paper. Students should plan to go start to finish on one sheet of paper, no ripping up and starting over. If they fill a piece of paper, give them another one. They are to cover the entire sheet of paper with drawings from different bags. The drawings should be as big as the size of the students' hands. Drawing small doesn't help them learn about lines.

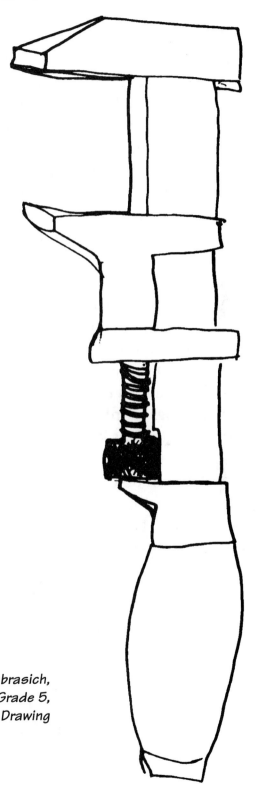

Sarah Dubrasich,
Grade 5,
Line Drawing

THE SETUP

Each student has a piece of paper and a felt pen. Give each student one bag with an object. Students may not look in the bag, they may not take the object out of the bag. The students are to reach in the bag and touch the object. They should roll the object around in their hands, feeling all sides of it. The students then draw the object from how it feels. They should examine the object for three to five minutes. Don't let them rush. Expect laughter. This exercise seems to titillate students a little. It's OK to laugh during art.

When they finish drawing an object from a bag, they may pass the bag to a neighbor or you may want to control the passing of the bags. Don't let the students rush from one bag to another. Some objects are easier than others to draw, so try to have five or six extra bags to interject into the passing order. This keeps all students drawing and no one waiting for an object. Leave all the objects in the bags on a table until the next day.

SUPPLIES

1. White paper, 18" x 24" or 12" x 18"
2. Felt pens, any color, thin tips
3. Small brown paper bags with one object inside each
4. Objects: spoon, light bulb, tea strainer, wrench, cord, jar, tennis ball, candle, screwdriver, plug

Sarah Dubrasich,
Grade 5,
Wrench, Line Drawing

12

GOALS

This exercise is about using senses other than the eyes. It is a way to explore texture and the sense of touch; it improves the students' ability to visualize. It is important for students to practice forming mental pictures using the imagination. Since there is no wrong way to do these drawings this exercise improves self-esteem and increases the students' self-confidence. Students evaluate and interpret information; they work as a team, sharing objects around the room.

Sarah Dubrasich,
Grade 5,
C-Clamp

SUMMARY OF STEPS

1. Hand out paper and felt pens.
2. Give each student a bag with an object inside.
3. Students may not look in the bag.
4. The students draw the object by feeling it.
5. Keep the drawings large.
6. Cover the whole piece of paper.

DRAWING FROM A BAG II

BRIEF OVERVIEW

There is no wrong way to do this exercise. The students should be encouraged to continue trying; remind them that practice makes perfect. Often a student, fearing failure will trace an object; this is actually a good way to learn about shape—especially if the students watch their hand going around the object. Students should, however, then try to draw the object without tracing. Drawing is all practice.

THE SETUP

Remove the objects from the bags and place them on a table. Have a few students at a time come up to the table and pick up one of the objects they drew the day before. The students then try to draw the object while looking at it. They may set the object on their desks in front of themselves or beside their papers. Once again the objects must be drawn as large as their hands. Each student, when finished, should return the first object and take whatever one is available that was drawn the day before. Cover the paper with objects; the drawings may overlap, run off the edge, or touch on the paper. The students may change the colors of their felt pens—one object drawn in red, one in black, the next one in green, and so on.

Sarah Dubrasich,
Grade 5,
Light Bulb

THE CRITIQUE AND GOALS

Hang up the drawings from Drawing from a Bag I and II and compare them. Ask the students which was more difficult to draw, which was more fun, which looks the best. Are they surprised that the drawings from touching the object often look as good as those from looking at the object?

This exercise improves hand-eye coordination. The students evaluate and interpret visual information; with each line they are making decisions.

SUMMARY STEPS

1. Take the objects out of the bags.
2. Place the objects on a table.
3. Let the students select one at a time.
4. Draw the objects while looking at them.
5. Cover the paper with drawings.

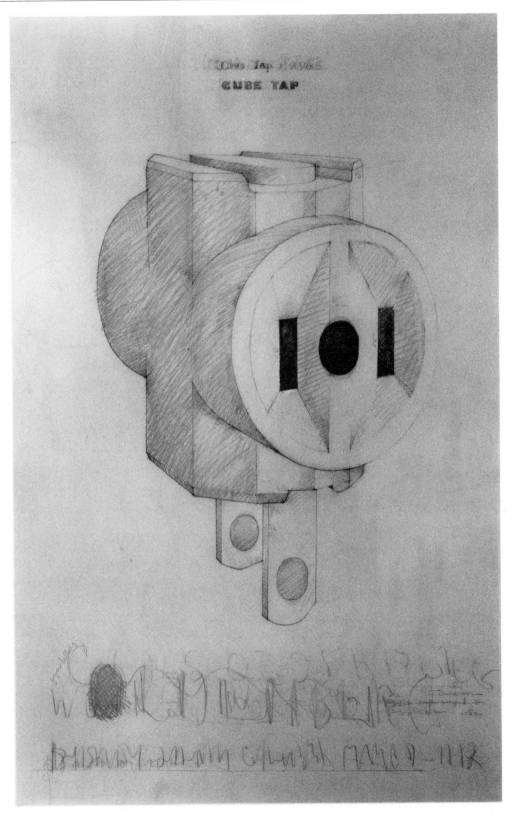

Claes Oldenburg, American, b. 1929, *Cube Tap (Plug)*, pencil on white wove paper, 1968.322. Photograph
© 1995. Courtesy of The Art Institute of Chicago. All rights reserved.

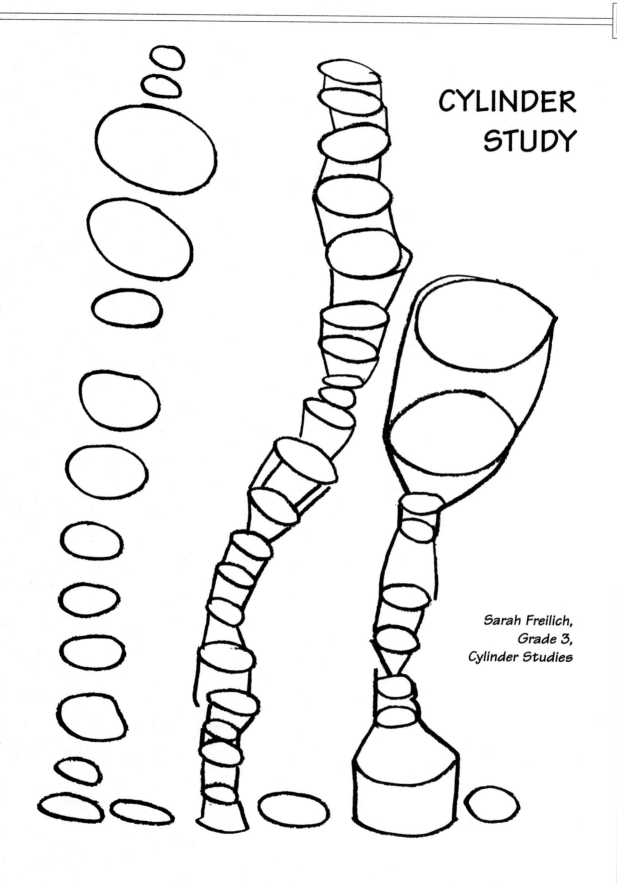

CYLINDER STUDY

Sarah Freilich,
Grade 3,
Cylinder Studies

3rd

2nd

1st

4th

Amanda Chiavini, Grade 5,
Cylinder Study

CYLINDER STUDY
Foundation Exercise

BRIEF OVERVIEW

Drawing objects to look round is a major problem—mostly because we think of round objects in terms of the circle, but the circle works to identify a shape only when one is looking directly into the center of a cup or vase or bowl. Once the students set the bowl down and look at it on a table, they have turned the circle some 90 degrees and the shape of the cup's opening is now that of an ellipse; therefore, it is important for the students to learn to make ellipses. There are a few rules in making ellipses.

The first rule: The corners or edges of the ellipse are round not pointed.

The second rule: The front curve is the same as the back curve, and the distance across each end of an ellipse should be the same at both ends.

The third rule: When drawing cylinders, the curve for the front edge at the top is the same as the surface curve for the entire shape all the way to the bottom ellipse.

The fourth rule: The circumference of the ellipses in a cylinder can vary from small to large. If the vase or cylinder has a wide-mouth top and small-footed base, merely change the size of the ellipse. At the same time, try to keep the curve the same up and down the vase. In this exercise it is particularly important that students not lean on their drawing hands. It is much easier to make good ellipses when the wrist has a full range of movement.

Example of Rule 1:

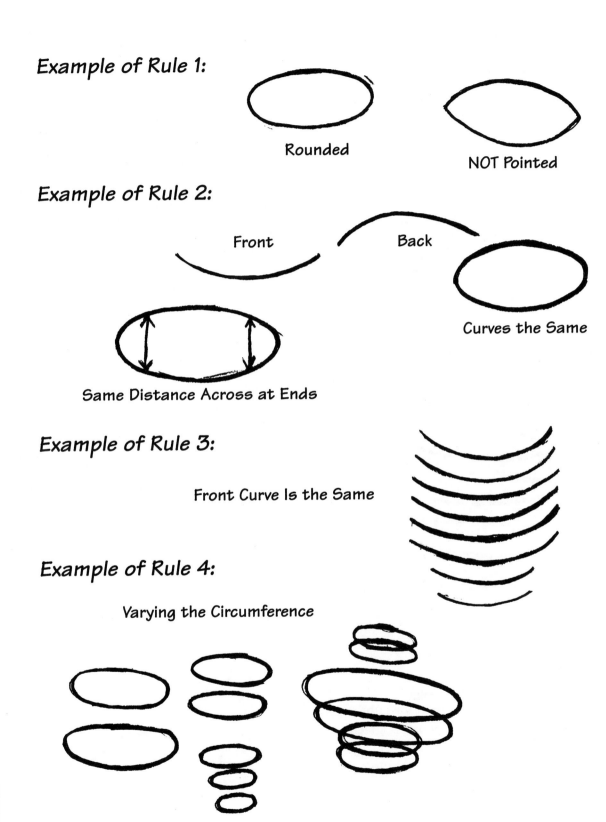

Rounded

NOT Pointed

Example of Rule 2:

Front

Back

Curves the Same

Same Distance Across at Ends

Example of Rule 3:

Front Curve Is the Same

Example of Rule 4:

Varying the Circumference

THE SETUP

The students start by drawing ellipses in rows and covering the page. The art on this and the following pages shows each step.

STEP 1

Draw the front curve first in one smooth, curving stroke. Next draw the back curve to match the front curve. A little trick to help this work is to use typing paper, which is thin and somewhat transparent. After the students draw the front curve, they should fold the paper over so they can see the curve through the paper and trace the curve to make the back curve. They may need to use a felt-tip pen.

Amanda Chiavini, Grade 5, Ellipses

STEP 2

Another way to construct an ellipse is to start the ellipse in the middle; draw the right curve then draw the left curve. The two halves attach in the middle. It is often better to construct the ellipse in two strokes than to try to achieve it in one circling motion.

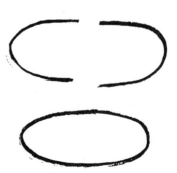

STEP 3

Make vertical rows of ellipses all the same size. Next make rows of ellipses where each two are the same size. Now make a row of ellipses that increase in size—the first four are small, followed by six medium-sized ellipses and then six large ellipses under them.

STEP 4

The students begin by connecting any two ellipses of the same size with a vertical line on their outside edges. Next, connect the two of the same size to the two larger ones below them with a diagonal line. Multi-shaped cylinders are formed by connecting these ellipses.

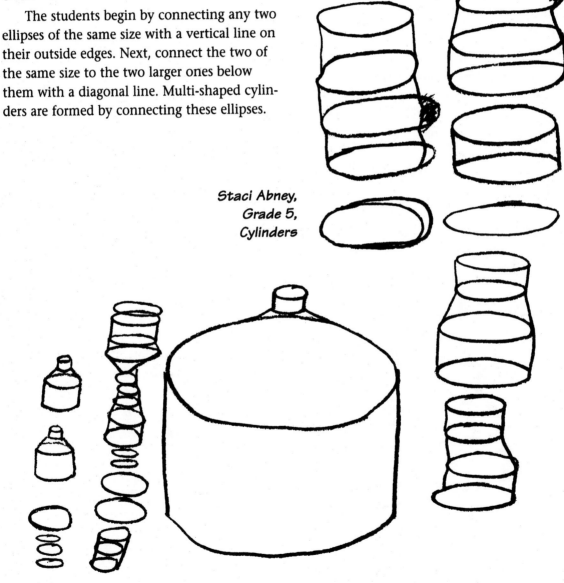

*Staci Abney,
Grade 5,
Cylinders*

Ben Verhoeven, Grade 6, Cylinders

STEP 5

Take two pencils of the same size. Holding the tips evenly together with the pencils upright, tie them together with a rubber band. Have the students make ellipses by drawing with both leads on the paper. Try to keep the front curve the same down the whole row. To form a volume, select any column of ellipses and connect the ellipses on the outside curve or edges. Take the pencil and reshape any curve that seems irregular. Little adjustments are always necessary.

STEP 6

This time, draw only the front curve with the double pencils. Vary the size of the ellipses in sections. There might be three very tiny curves, followed by six larger curves, followed by four curves smaller than the first six. This would probably look like a fat vase when the outside edges are connected with lines and diagonals. The outside line may be curved to fit along the outside edge of the ellipses. This is one of the adjustments previously mentioned. When the outside lines are connected they may need to be moved in and out to shape the form.

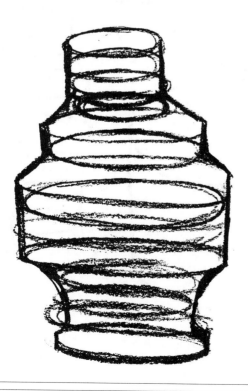

GOALS

This exercise improves hand-eye coordination and perception. Students are involved in the creative thinking process with decision—making and listening skills equally challenged.

Eigendruck   E L Kirchner

Ernst Ludwig Kirchner, German, 1880–1938, *Head of Young Man*, drypoint, 1925, 30.2 x 25 cm, Print and
Drawing Purchase Account, Purchased from Robert Light, Santa Barbara, California, 1966.30. Photograph
© 1995, The Art Institute of Chicago. All rights reserved.

CYLINDER II—A DRAWING EXERCISE
Foundation Exercise

BRIEF OVERVIEW

After the students have practiced making ellipses and forming cylinders from the inside out, they can apply what they've learned and use their imaginations to make a drawing. This exercise is not from seeing but from imagining.

THE SETUP

This is an exercise to design a fruit bowl. With the HB pencil draw a large ellipse on a piece of paper a third of the way down from the top. Moving down the paper four or five inches, draw a small ellipse. Connect the outside curves of both

ellipses on both sides. This form now resembles a large bowl to which fruit can be added. Draw in the fruit from the front of the bowl to the back. In the example, the grapes are in the front. Grapes are just a series of overlapping small circles that drape over the front edge. Oranges are just circles with a dark dot for the top indentation. Apples have a large curved *M* shape on top.

To separate the forms, have the students hatch one side or the bottom of each form with the 6B pencil. Hatching lines are individual lines that can be drawn horizontally, vertically or diagonally. They should be drawn close together and attached to some edge of the form. Hatching creates value change in the drawing. The bowl can be located on a ground with shadow underneath.

SUMMARY OF STEPS

1. Draw a large ellipse.
2. Draw a small ellipse four inches down.
3. Connect the ellipses.
4. Stack fruit in the large ellipse.
5. Darken the bottom of the forms.
6. Erase unnecessary marks.

Have a couple of white plastic erasers in your pocket. At the end of the drawing, let the students erase any smudges or really annoying marks on the drawings. Stand there while they erase, pick up the eraser and move to the next student who requests an eraser. Tell them in advance that all erasing will be done at the end of the drawing, so they should draw very lightly until they are sure they have things where they want them. Only then should they darken the lines on the drawing.

GOALS

This exercise provides students with an opportunity to put a newly learned technique into practice; they must transfer theory into practical application.

Caleb Jones, Grade 4
Pencil Drawing

CYLINDER III—HANDLES AND SPOUTS

Foundation Exercise

Once the students have the idea of constructing a cylinder from a series of ellipses, they will need some additional help with handles. For a pitcher, first construct the body and the top with an opening.

The handle is made from two lines off the top, which at one point meet and cross each other (Diagram I).

Next bring one of the lines down to where the handle meets the body of the pitcher. Now draw a second line inside the first one for the inside of the handle (Diagram II).

Diagram I	Diagram II	Diagram III

There are two types of spouts. The spout shown in Diagram III is constructed by drawing a triangular shape off the top ellipse and then connecting the outside tip with a curved line to the pitcher's neck. The other spout is shown in Diagram IV and V. Draw two ellipses the same size, one on the pitcher and one above the pitcher where the spout ends. Connect the outside curves of the ellipses.

A plate or a dish is an ellipse with another ellipse inside it. To increase the definition of the shape, use a double line on the front edge. This shows the thickness of the plate.

Cameron Clancey Decoster, Grade 4/5, Charcoal

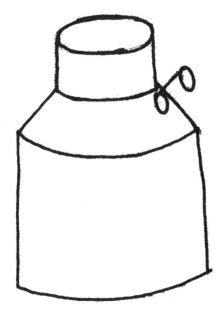

Diagram IV

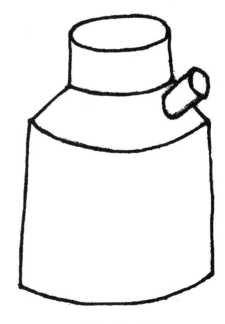

Diagram V

OUTLINE DRAWING

BRIEF OVERVIEW

Before the students start to draw, have them hold the object in one hand directly in front of themselves. Have them follow the shape of the object by drawing with their fingers in the air. They should be looking at the object for any change in texture, shape, or material. For example, material changes would be a wooden handle for a metal tool, or a ribbed metal end for a light bulb. Those changes are indicated by lines separating the sections in the drawing. In this air drawing, the students follow the outside shape, twisting and turning their fingers, drawing all they are seeing in the air. The more information their eyes and other senses have, the easier it is to draw an object.

Sarah Dubrasich,
Grade 5,
Scissors

SUPPLIES

1. 18" x 24" white 60–80 lb. drawing paper

2. Felt pens—all colors, fat and thin tips

3. Simple objects: light bulbs, tennis balls, spoons, wrenches, hammers, toothbrushes, sunglasses, plugs, scissors, screwdrivers, pliers

THE SETUP

The students start with a few felt pens and one object. They are to make a simple line, drawing no smaller than their hands on the paper. Students should look at the object, continue to feel the shape, and then draw a line that follows the outside contour of the object. When there's a groove, draw in with the line. If the form bulges, draw out with the line. Start the drawing either from the top of the object or the bottom, making the line follow the contour of the object.

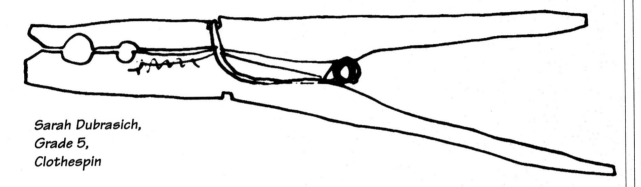

Sarah Dubrasich,
Grade 5,
Clothespin

The students may use any color felt pen. They may place the objects anywhere on the page. They should cover the page with drawings. They may turn the paper upside down or sideways if necessary to fit all the objects. Don't let students draw on the back of the paper. It is better to give them another sheet of paper if they have filled their first one.

When the students finish with an object, they should pass it to a neighbor. Because some objects are easier than others, have a few extra objects to slip into the sequence, that

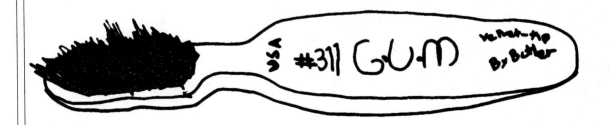

Sarah Dubrasich,
Grade 5,
Toothbrush

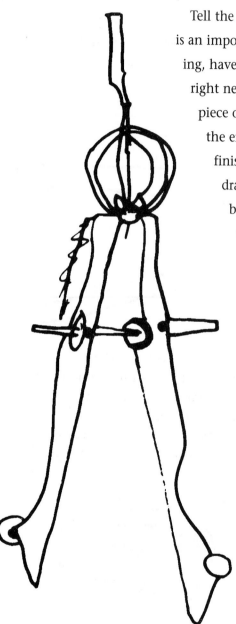

way no one will be sitting and waiting for an object.

Tell the students not to cross out any drawings. Every drawing is an important part of learning to draw. If they don't like a drawing, have them draw the object again on the same piece of paper right next to the one they don't like. Don't give them a second piece of paper to start over. Once they start, they continue to the end; starting over doesn't help. Tell them that once they finish the first drawing they can do another. When they draw a line that they feel is wrong, it is really good, because now they know they don't want the line to be there, and they can move the line left or right off the bad line, placing the line where they prefer it to be. If they erase the bad line, they must start all over guessing where to put the first or "right" line. In drawing the compass Sarah used this replacement line process. The line crossed out to the left was her first line.

GOALS

This exercise develops visual awareness and perception and improves hand-eye coordination. It also improves drawing skills and line quality.

Sarah Dubrasich,
Grade 5,
Compass

SUMMARY STEPS

1. Hand out paper and felt pens.
2. Students draw the contour shape of the object in the air.
3. Students draw the object's outline as big as a hand.
4. Students pass the object to another and draw a new one.

Marino Marini, Italian 1901–1980, *Horse and Rider,* 1953, India ink and gouache on paper, 24 1/2" x 16 15/16". Muscarelle Museum of Art. Gift of Mr. and Mrs. Ralph Lamberson. College of William and Mary in Virginia.

RHYTHM DRAWINGS

Andrew Thomson,
Grade 3,
Paintbrushes

RHYTHM DRAWINGS

SUPPLIES

1. 18" x 24" white drawing paper

2. Multicolored thin-tip felt pens

3. Simple objects: light bulbs, a tennis ball, wrenches, a screwdriver, a toothbrush, a can of hair spray

BRIEF OVERVIEW

This drawing involves making some decisions in advance. Each student selects one object to draw, then decides in what direction the objects will be arranged on the paper. Possible arrangement choices include placing the objects horizontally from one side of the paper to the other; overlapping the objects in a circular pattern. The student can start with a small drawing of the object and increase the size of the object in each overlapping drawing. They can also make an overall page arrangement. Three of these possible arrangements are shown here.

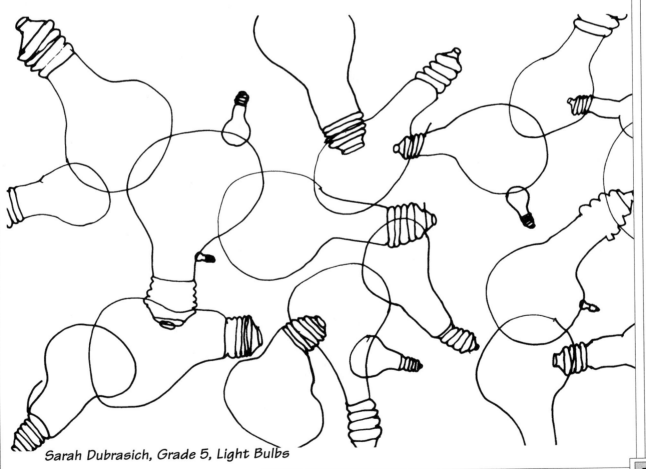

Sarah Dubrasich, Grade 5, Light Bulbs

THE SETUP

Each student draws a simple outline of the object. In this initial drawing, a little detail on the object is good, but too much is hard to repeat. They draw the object again, and this second drawing must overlap the first drawing somewhere on its perimeter. The students continue to draw the object, each drawing overlapping the outline prior to it. The objects should be drawn to cross the page from side to side or top to bottom in whatever pattern the student has selected. These drawings should either fill the page or run off two sides to most effectively get the feeling of the object's moving. It is often helpful to rotate the paper, turn it sideways or upside-down to draw the object more easily. Overlapping and repeating the same drawing can get confusing.

The number of pens used will also affect the results. The students may change the color of their felt pens with each outline. They may use one color or use just two colors. Once the students have covered the page, the drawing is done.

CRITIQUE AND GOALS

Overlapping shapes is the beginning of perspective drawing in that overlapping shapes create space. The flat space of the paper is now seemingly three-dimensional. The discussion should focus on the motion in the drawings. Ask the students if they notice any one object or is it hard to focus on one? This exercise build visual awareness. Students must plan the composition and make decisions.

Sarah Freilich, Grade 3, Wrenches

Gino Severini, Italian 1883–1966, *Train Crossing a Street,* charcoal with black conté crayon and touches of black chalk over graphite on cream wove paper. c. 1915/16, 55.2 x 46.4 cm. Alfred Stieglitz Collection, 1949.903. Photograph © 1995, The Art Institute of Chicago. All rights reserved.

GEOMETRIC LINE DRAWING

SUPPLIES

1. 11" x 17" white drawing paper

2. Felt pens, all colors, fat and thin tips

3. Pencil (HB) and rulers

4. Simple objects (same as those in the line drawing exercise)

THE SETUP

STEP 1

Students select four or five objects to draw on the paper in light pencil outlines. The goal is to fill the page with objects. Pick one object that is round. Draw one object touching the top and bottom edge of the paper; one going off the edge; and draw one diagonally across the paper. Make the drawings large; small drawings are hard to work with. Don't bother erasing misshapen drawings; all distortion of the shape is acceptable and will hardly be noticed when the exercise is completed. The drawings of the objects may overlap. After they have all the objects drawn on the paper, let them erase lines that are too dark to be covered with felt-tip pen or are really bothersome to them.

STEP 2

Using the ruler, divide the paper in fourths with an HB or light pencil. Next divide each quadrant with a diagonal line. In the example, there are a couple of choices for dividing the quadrants, they may draw a line from the center to the corner in each quadrant or draw a line from the center point to center point on each side.

STEP 3

Using felt tip pens the students color the divisions in the drawing. Each color stays within an outlined section. Change the color of the felt pen when the students must cross a line. They cannot cross a line using the same color. The line referred to in the rule can be one of the division lines or a line that is part of the outline of an object. The colors will repeat throughout the drawing. The white of the paper can be left in any area that is surrounded by colors. (but try to avoid placing the same color in two sections side by side.)

Step 1: Draw simple outlines of four or five objects to fill the page.

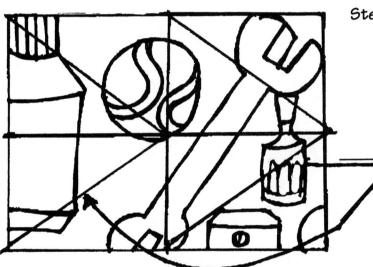

Step 2: Divide the page into fourths, then divide each quadrant with a diagonal (optional direction of line below).

Diagonal Options

Step 3: Color in the sections of the drawing, alternating colors at each line.

CRITIQUE

The students can see how color affects perception. Some areas of the drawing will appear closer while others will seem to recede into the space. Do light or dark colors advance? Do light or dark colors recede? Discuss how the color divisions affect perception. What has happened to the two-dimensional space of the paper?

This is a beginning step in understanding how artists make abstract art. Abstraction often comes from and refers to something very real. In abstraction, reality is transformed.

GOALS

This exercise makes an easy curriculum tie to math. It develops critical thinking skills, increases perception, and involves decision-making skills. In addition, the basic learning skills of listening and following instructions are very important to complete this exercise.

SUMMARY OF STEPS

1. Students select four or five objects.
2. They draw them lightly on the paper.
3. They should draw large outlined shapes.
4. Then divide the paper in fourths.
5. Then divide each quadrant diagonally.
6. The students color each section keeping one color inside each bordered area and changing the color when they cross a line.

Giacomo Balla, Italian 1871–1958, *Motivo con la parola buon Appetito, (Motif with the Word Good Appetite)*, 1915, watercolor and pencil on paper, 8 7/8" diam. San Francisco Museum of Modern Art.
Gift of Dr. and Mrs. Domenico Manzone, 81.250.

Alberto Giacometti, Swiss, 1901–1966, *Portrait of the Artist's Wife Annette,* pencil on ivory wove paper, 1949, 63.8 x 49.9 cm. Adelaide C. Brown Fund, 1955.636. Photograph © 1995, The Art Institute of Chicago. All rights reserved.

SCRIBBLED LINE DRAWING

BRIEF OVERVIEW

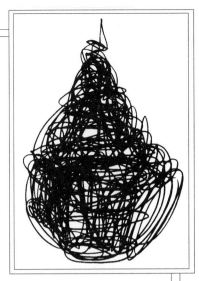

This type of drawing is also referred to as *line gesture* or *mass gesture*. It is used to draw and describe an object from the inside to the outside. The students will use thick, thin, wide, narrow, heavy, and light lines in this drawing.

It is important that students pick one view of the subject and not move their heads while drawing. The lines of the drawing follow the movement of the eyes as they examine the object. As the eyes move, so does the pen. The pen is kept in constant contact with the paper, never lifting off the surface. The lines will become tangled and overlapped, wrapping the form up as if it was wrapped in string. The lines look like a scribble but they are not meaningless, because the student is thinking and drawing every inch of the surface of the form. Each line is a record of a thought.

The pressure on the drawing tool is important. Start with very light pressure; as the eyes move out from the center, have the students vary the pressure. Where there seems to be tension in the object—a crease, fold, or dent—or where the shape seems heaviest or darkest (probably on the underside or the side turned away from the light), the students increase the pressure, darkening the lines. Making these judgments about the direction of the line, the amount of pressure to use and where to go next is the first step in creative thinking.

Have the students try to pretend that they are drawing on the object's surface, not outlining the form. Pretend the pen is actually on the object. Which way do they need to twist and turn the pen to move across the surface of the object to get to the edge and back? They should also use circular and elliptical strokes, pretending to draw the back of the object as well as the front. They are to continue making lines until the drawing of the object is covered with lines. These lines fill the entire surface, shaping the object more as a mass than an outline.

THE SETUP

SUPPLIES

1. 12" x 18" white drawing paper

2. Ball point pens or fine-point felt-tip pens

3. Subjects: apples, eggplant, squash, oranges, grapefruit, pears, pineapples, or any classroom pet such as bunnies, hamsters, or mice

Each student may have one object, or they may work together in groups. Groups of four work well. Four desks can be pulled into a circle around one empty desk on which the object can be placed. It is best to have the object directly in front of the students. If the classroom has tables, have the students sit across from each other with the object in the middle placed the object in front of the students.

To draw animals, I have had students sit quietly around the cage. An active pet may be too difficult for this exercise. The students should look at the subject, pick a starting point at its imagined center, place the pen on the paper, and begin drawing lines that circle the form, avoiding the contour or the object's outline. They will start with light pressure on the pen. The pen follows the eyes as they roam across the surface of the object. Don't lift the pen off the paper. The line moves across the object's surface from the back to the front, from the top to the bottom. The lines go around the object, circling it as in the cylinder exercise. Keep the line moving to describe the object. The line may circle, overlap, turn, and twist around on the paper. The object will appear to be wrapped in lines. Increase the pressure on the pen for shaded areas, dents, folds, or creases. This drawing should be a dense mass of multiple overlapping lines. The outside edge will be fuzzy with no definite line.

CRITIQUE

Hang up the drawings. It is always better to look at drawings on the wall. What has happened to the flat surface of the paper? What areas seem to come forward; which seem to go back into the paper? Is there a difference between the light and dark areas? Can they tell anything about the surface texture? Does it feel like a volume? How heavy does the object feel?

GOALS

This exercise is excellent for hand-eye coordination and critical thinking. With every stroke of the pen, the students make a decision. The students must evaluate and interpret the information received by their eyes. This takes patience.

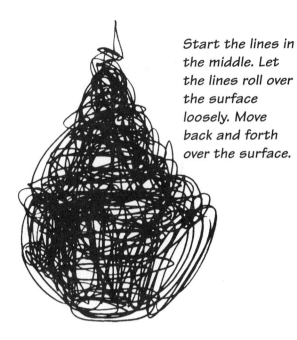

Start the lines in the middle. Let the lines roll over the surface loosely. Move back and forth over the surface.

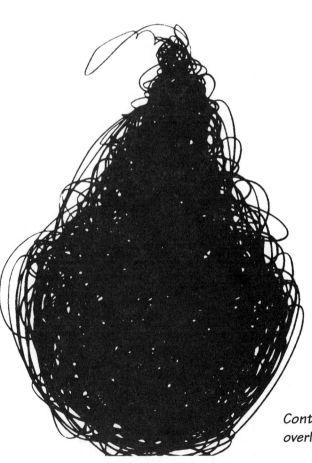

Follow the roundness of the form. Direct the lines as the form is leaning.

Continue overlapping lines.

CONTINUOUS LINE DRAWING

BRIEF OVERVIEW

The line in the continuous line drawing is unbroken from beginning to end. The drawing tool stays on the paper through the entire drawing never lifting off the surface. As in the scribbled line drawing, the line can go across the object's surface to get to the other side.

Set up a large still life on a table in front of the room or put the students' desks in a circle, with the still life table in the middle of the room. All students must be able to see some section of the still life. They do not have to draw the entire still life. They need only concentrate on one section.

Have them draw whatever number of objects will fit on the paper. Have them concentrate on one object at a time. They start with the object that is in front of all the others they intend to draw. The front object should be clear of any other object overlapping it. Draw the outline and interior details of the first object without lifting the pen; continue the line across the empty space (the negative space) between the first object and the second object. Then continue in this manner, adding on one object after another, filling the paper from side to side.

Have them look at where the base of the second object is in relation to the first object. Are the bases even, or is one further back or off to the side? This is important to think about. If the base of the second object is behind the first, the line connecting them across the empty space should go diagonally, or up the paper a little. To show that some objects are behind others, they are placed up the page drawing the base lines one behind another. The examples of other students' continuous line drawings may help explain these directions.

The students must keep their eyes on the subject that they are drawing. Have them try to imagine that the point of the drawing tool is in actual contact with the subject. Their eyes should not move across the objects faster than they can draw them. They may occasionally glance at their papers to check their location and then return their gaze to the still life.

SETTING UP A STILL LIFE

Place the objects on the table with space between them. Arrange the objects front to back on the table. Some of the objects should overlap. String the objects out across the table, offering the students a choice of sections. Use simple vases, bottles, oranges, teapots, and candle holders. You may place fabric under the objects or behind them. White fabric under the objects will reflect the cast shadows. Flowered fabric in the background will offer the students some pattern to follow in the drawing. The secondhand store is a marvelous resource for still life objects.

THE SETUP

The students begin the drawing with the object in the front. They place the pen on the paper and begin a line around the first object. This should be a free-flowing continuous line. This line will connect the objects and the space between them. Since the students cannot lift the pen, they are to draw a line across the space that separates the objects. The students should cover the entire surface of the paper, allowing the drawing to go off at least three sides of the paper. They should vary the weight of the line, pressing harder in those areas where there is a shadow.

GOALS

This exercise builds hand-eye coordination. It increases critical, creative thinking skills and enhances decision-making skills. Students must evaluate and interpret information to describe the space they are drawing.

SUPPLIES

1. 18" x 24" white paper

2. Thin black felt-tip pens or ball-point pens

3. Still life setup: a vase, coffeepot, suitcase, bottles, plastic fruit, baskets, real fruit or plants, or other found objects

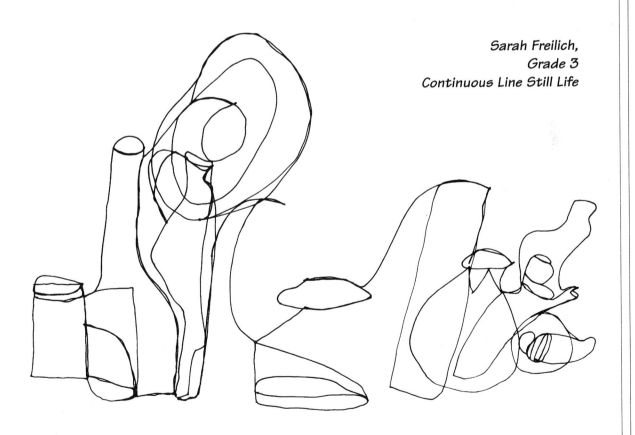

Sarah Freilich,
Grade 3
Continuous Line Still Life

Tamara Mlady, Grade 4, Continuous Line Still Life

CRITIQUE

The students have now drawn across negative space as well as positive space. The empty space is equally important in a drawing. It is important to think about the space between objects. The continuous line increases the complexity of the drawing. Discuss how they perceive the objects in the drawing compared with how they perceive the objects on the table. Are the objects recognizable? Have the objects been abstracted?

SUMMARY OF STEPS

1. The drawing tool is a free-flowing pen.
2. The line is unbroken.
3. The pen stays in constant contact with the paper.
4. The line may cross the object's surface.
5. The line must be drawn across the empty space.
6. Fill the entire paper.
7. The hand follows the eyes; don't rush.
8. The weight of the line will vary.
9. The lines will overlap.

Lindsay Bolerjack, Grade 4, Continuous Line Drawing

ILLUSTRATING SCIENCE WORDS

SUPPLIES

1. Paper or tag board

2. Colored pencils, felt-tip pens, paint, collage materials

3. Dictionaries

BRIEF OVERVIEW

Each academic discipline has a specific vocabulary. It is often difficult for students to understand the meaning of words new to them. This exercise helps students understand the meaning of new words by illustrating and visualizing them. Students look the word up, write the definition, and make a drawing that illustrates the concept and the word. They decide what format to use and what materials to use in their project.

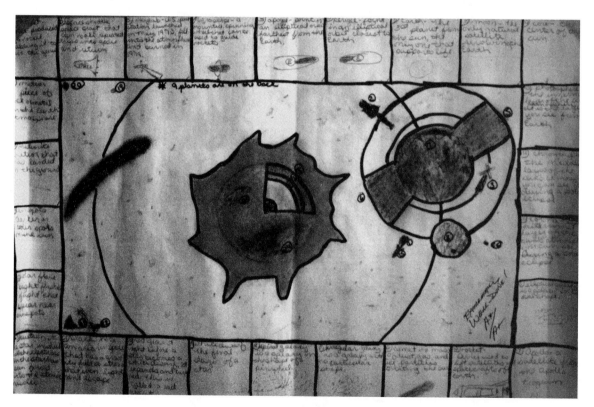

Artist Unknown, Grade 7, Illustrating Science Words

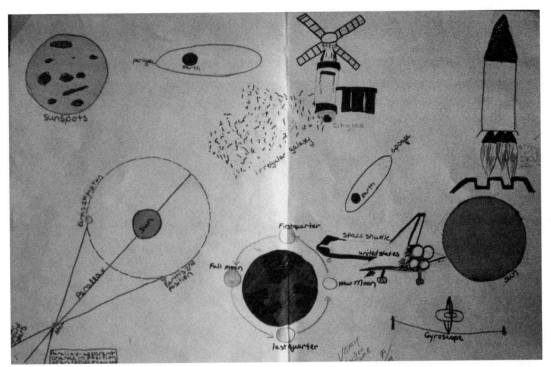

Artist Unknown, Grade 7, Illustrating Science Words

THE SETUP

Compile a list of words and concepts the students are to research. Give them the list and their deadline to finish the project.

Set out the classroom art supplies and dictionaries. Let the students choose between felt-tip pens, crayons, colored pencils, watercolors, tempera paints, collage materials, tag board, construction paper, or whatever you have for art supplies. In this way the project is entirely the students,' from start to finish. All decisions for the composition are the students'. Each student may arrange the words and concepts differently and each may pick different materials.

CRITIQUE

Display the students' finished projects. This exercise offers a good example for talk about individual difference in creating a work of art. Each student takes a different approach to the problem. All the students had the same instructions, but no two drawings are the same.

Ask the students to explain how they made their choices for layout and materials. Ask them what they learned about the words and concepts. What new techniques did they discover in their materials; what happened that they did not expect?

GOALS

This exercise teaches students to solve problems and make decisions. They appreciate, and understand, the value of individual difference. The project builds self-esteem and self-discipline. Students must evaluate and interpret information.

SECTION TWO:
Value and Modeling

1. Value—A Discussion of Black and White: Foundation Exercise

2. Chiaroscuro I: Foundation Exercise

3. Chiaroscuro II: Foundation Exercise

4. Reversed Charcoal: Dark to Light

5. Simple Still Life in Charcoal: Foundation Exercise

6. Wet Charcoal

7. Cross-Hatching Practice: Foundation Exercise

8. Cross-Hatching a Still Life: Creating Value

9. Pencil Still Life: Rubbed and Erased

10. Warm-up for Ink Drawing: Foundation Exercise

11. Building Ink Washes

12. Ink Line Drawing

Elizabeth Allen, Grade 5, Charcoal

A DISCUSSION OF VALUE

Foundation Exercise

Value change is the gradation from light to dark across a form and from dark to light. Light and dark may be determined by local color (the actual color of the object). The direction and amount of light falling on the object also determines where the light and dark values fall. Objects may be green and orange and still have the same value, but if one object is dark green and the other is light orange, they are different values. When the color changes from light orange to dark orange, we experience value change. Value change is very important in a drawing. Drawings without value change will look flat or more patternlike. Without a change from light to dark an interior space will be compressed and seem shallow. In still life drawing the foreground is often lighter in value than the background, whereas in landscape drawing the foreground trees or buildings will be much darker than the lighter hills seen faintly in the background.

The ten-step value scale shows the range of possible lights and darks. A drawing of sharp value contrasts uses the extreme ends of the scale, placing the very lightest and very darkest together. Using the middle values creates a subtle soft effect. Placing a cast shadow under a form locates and attaches it to the ground upon which it is sitting.

Value is the primary means of organizing any composition. It is value change that directs the viewer's eye around the drawing. Value change is used to describe and separate the planes of a structure, to interpret the direction and amount of light that is falling on a form, and to imply the space of a room—informing us as to how much distance there is from the front to the back of a room. Value can also create a sense of heaviness, describing the weight of an object.

The decision of where to use light and dark may depend on translating actual light falling through space on forms or it may be entirely made up by the artist to manipulate the drawing for creative reasons.

In Chiaroscuro I the students practice controlling light and dark on a circle in terms of the Renaissance formula of how light falls on organic or round forms. They are not looking at light on an actual form yet. By practicing creating value changes, they begin to understand where, why, and how lights and darks can be manipulated to create volume.

All materials have limitations and different characteristics. Charcoal and pencils have very different ranges in value, which will become evident to the students in the following exercises. The exercises in the value section look at how actual light falls on form and how it is interpreted.

Ten Step Value Scale

In a classroom, unless you can darken the windows, focus a floodlight on a still life, and sit the exact distance at the exact angle needed, it is difficult to see perfect separations between light gray, gray, medium gray, dark gray, and finally black. The students must determine where the value will change across each object in the drawing as well as in the foreground and background space of the drawing.

It is also difficult to determine value change and where the value breaks because we don't see gray, light gray, dark gray, we see an object as dark or light orange. It is the light and dark of color that the students must interpret into the ten step value scale. It may help the students to interpret light if they see a color photo that has been photocopied. The photocopy machine makes the same decisions regarding dark and light that the students must make, only it has an electronic program to do it and the students must use their senses, knowledge, and experience.

The values and tones in a drawing may be created by rubbing, smudging, erasing, stippling, or layering washes one on top of another. Each time the student adds a layer, the value darkens. Younger students will be satisfied with one or two layers while older students have the patience to persist and work the drawing a little more. Each experience will improve the students' level of perception.

Value Study, College Student, Drawing I

Dave Sahr, Grade 5, Charcoal

CHIAROSCURO I
Foundation Exercise

BRIEF OVERVIEW

Chiaroscuro is an Italian word, coined during the Renaissance, which means light and dark. The word itself can be divided into *chiaro,* meaning light and *oscuro,* meaning dark. The term *shading* may be a more familiar term for defining light-into-dark on form, or one might refer to it as *value change*. The light effects of chiaroscuro are for cylinders and round forms only. Light operates differently on geometric or square forms. This exercise examines how to create the effect of light falling on forms, and in so doing, to create the illusion of volume, space, and depth in drawing.

It is important for students to think of drawing as an illusion, not a reality, because their drawings are their interpretations of what they are seeing. To improve their drawings, they must improve their levels of perception and begin to pay greater attention to details. They must also improve their hand-eye coordination skills by practicing.

The students must accept whatever they produce. They should understand that learning to draw depends on their personal interpretation of space, and that each drawing is an important step toward making better representations. When they can apply the formulas and rules of drawing to interpret what they see three-dimensionally onto a two-dimensional surface, drawing will become easier. Interpretating space is not something we do naturally; we learn to represent space on a flat piece of paper.

To understand the problem of translating space from three dimensions to two dimensions, start a lesson by holding up a vase and asking the students if it is two-dimensional or three-dimensional. Then hold up a piece of paper and ask them the same question—two- or three-dimensional? They really haven't thought much about this difference, so point out to them that they are creating an illusion. The paper has no volume or depth; they will invent it.

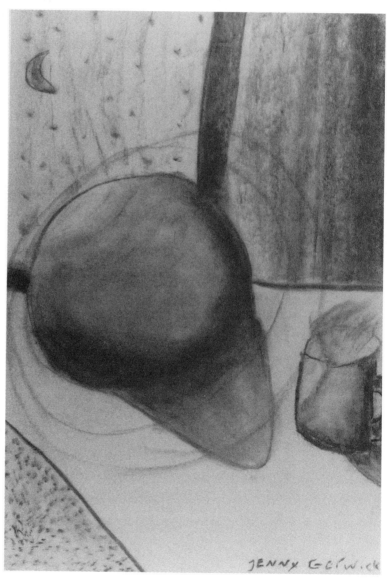

Jenny Gerwick, Grade 4/5, Charcoal with Erased Circles

THE SETUP

Charcoal drawing is an additive and subtractive process in which value is controlled from very light to medium gray to dark gray and black. When you add more charcoal, the values get darker. Rubbing out charcoal results in lighter values. The students may use a finger, a tissue wrapped around the finger, or the chamois to rub the charcoal. There are no mistakes in charcoal drawing, as any area that needs to be changed is simply wiped out with the hand or the chamois and drawn again.

Each student has one piece of paper and a piece of vine charcoal (vine is soft and they may well need another piece to complete the lesson). The purpose of this exercise is to practice using charcoal and making value changes on a circle.

The students draw a large circle on the white paper. If they want to change the shape they take the tissue, the chamois, or their hand and rub the charcoal into the paper. A small, light silhouette of the line will be left but it is not important; tell them to ignore it. Artists leave lines lightly in the background of their drawings all the time. It is hard to erase charcoal lines, usually we just cover them up (Diagram I). Jenny Gerwick's drawing on the previous page is a good example of leaving lines.

The students decide on which side the light will fall on the ball. It is an arbitrary decision, as they are making up the value changes; this is for practice. Then they should indicate where the light falls on the ball's top—first with small dots circling the first place the light strikes the ball or the **hot spot** (Diagram II).

Holding the charcoal between the thumb and the first two fingers, start at the bottom of the circle and wipe or rub the charcoal back and forth on its side and the edge, covering the lower half of the circle. This cross-hatching stroke—twisting and turning the piece of charcoal on half of the circle—creates the dark value. The strokes layered on top of each other will make a rich dark. Becca Henriksen's drawing, page 62 has a strong medium-to-dark division.

Now wrap the tissue around the index finger to rub the charcoal stretching it up and then around the top of the circle (Diagram III). The rubbing moves the charcoal across the middle of the ball. The students may use their fingers, the tissue the chamois, or the stump.

SUPPLIES

1. 12" x 18" white drawing paper
2. 12" x 18" tag board
3. 1" piece of vine charcoal
4. 1 section of compressed charcoal
5. Watercolor brush
6. Cup of water
7. Tissues
8. Rag or paper towels (optional)
9. Chamois
10. Stump

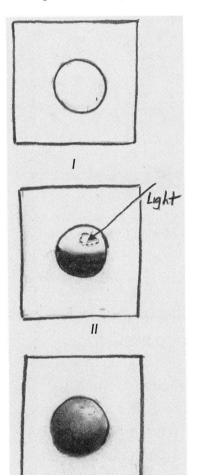

I

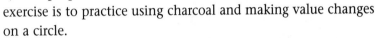

II

III

Diagrams I, II, and III
Chiaroscuro

The chamois can be used to erase marks made by vine charcoal, and it can be used on charcoal and conté to lighten values or to blend tones. The stump is also used to blend tones.

Leave a white spot for the hot spot at the top of the circle, which is now surrounded by light gray. The rubbing and wiping while moving the charcoal to create the light values on top will also lighten the value of the black on the bottom to a gray. Add another layer of charcoal over the bottom third to improve the contrast between the top and the bottom. The desired result is black at the bottom, gray in the middle, and light gray on top with a hot spot.

USING THE KNEADED ERASER

The kneaded eraser absorbs charcoal if you press it into the area to be removed and rub the area gently. Once the eraser is dirty, clean it by stretching it or pulling it like a piece of taffy and then folding it back into a ball. It is better not to pull the eraser completely apart. It should be stretched just enough to pull the charcoal area out; then return it to a ball.

USING THE PLASTIC ERASER

This eraser will lift charcoal out when you rub over it. When the plastic eraser gets dirty, it stops erasing and begins smearing the charcoal. Simply rub the dirty area of the eraser on a clean piece of scratch paper until it is clean, and the charcoal will be removed.

Blake Shaw-Phillips, Grade 5, Charcoal

ADDING A SHADOW TO THE BOTTOM

The shadow falls away from the ball at the angle of the light, so if the hot spot or the light circle at the top is on the right side of the ball, the shadow will be on the left side. Start the shadow on the bottom edge of the circle. The end of the circle and the beginning of the shadow are the same line. There is no distance between the two.

If there is space between the shadow and the ball it will float, which is also fun to do. The students might like to make a smaller ball and place the shadows at a distance from its bottom edge—just to see what happens.

Becca Henriksen, Grade 4/5, Charcoal

USING COMPRESSED CHARCOAL

Compressed charcoal comes in block or stick form. The square shape allows the students to draw with the end, flat side or edge beween two sides. It is much darker than vine, less dusty and harder to erase. It can be mixed with vine by adding a layer of compressed to a layer of vine, or it can be used alone. When compressed charcoal is rubbed it becomes a rich black as opposed to the graying effect rubbing has on vine. Use compressed charcoal in areas of the drawing to be the blackest. It is blacker than vine by a good deal. Introduce compressed charcoal only after students have used the vine.

Compressed charcoal can be used with water. Using the tag board make different marks with the charcoal stick. Dip a quill or watercolor brush in water and brush over the marks. Then draw more marks with the dirty brush on the paper. These washed marks will be more gray than black and the brush marks will also be light gray.

Draw another circle and using the compressed charcoal cover the bottom half of the circle then take a brush and dip it in the water. Wipe the wet brush over a small area of compressed charcoal and then use the dirty brush to create the lighter values on top of the circle. The brush may be dipped back in the water to maintain the flow of the wash. Keep the bristles damp. Once compressed charcoal dries, the students can mark on top of the area again with either vine or compressed charcoal. Have the students experiment making different layers of compressed charcoal. In a drawing both vine and compressed charcoal may be used together. It is best to experiment with them one at a time first.

Sarah Freilich's drawing on the following page uses both vine and compressed charcoal. She used the vine first on the ball and on the foreground. Then she rubbed compressed charcoal across the background. She then took a brush and washed over the area now darkest behind the ball. The grid in the foreground is compressed charcoal drawn on a layer of vine charcoal. The shadow is also compressed charcoal.

SUMMARY OF STEPS

1. Hand out paper and vine charcoal.
2. Ask the students to draw a circle.
3. Establish the direction of light source.
4. Start at the bottom of the circle and rub the charcoal on the lower half of the circle.
5. Rub the charcoal from the bottom to the middle and up to the top with tissue or stump.
6. Reinforce bottom third of drawing with another layer of charcoal to darken.
7. Add a shadow.
8. Experiment with compressed charcoal and water.

GOALS

To develop a better understanding of the material properties of charcoal. To practice making a range of grays and moving from light to dark. To see how light falling on form is translated into charcoal which is limited to a gray scale that goes from white to black. Authorities speculate that the human eye can easily separate approximately nine differences in value.

Sarah Freilich, Grade 3, Charcoal

John Noon, Grade 5, Charcoal

CHIAROSCURO II

Foundation Exercise

SUPPLIES

1. Drawing from Chiaroscuro I
2. Vine charcoal
3. Compressed charcoal
4. Water and brush
5. Fixative
6. Tissues
7. Chamois

BRIEF OVERVIEW

Exercises I and II have been separated so that each teacher can do this lesson in the time available. If time permits, this lesson continues Chiaroscuro I, using the same setup, the same supplies, and the same drawing.

THE SETUP

After the students have drawn and shaded the ball, they now consider the background and the foreground space of their drawing. First the students add a horizontal line at the midpoint of the ball and on both sides. It now looks as if the ball sits on a table or perhaps the floor. To the background they may add a window—perhaps with a landscape outside the window with mountains, lakes, roads, cars, or clouds. The student drawings on pp. 56, 58, 60, and 62 are good examples of the possibilities.

By adding another horizontal line a half inch above the horizontal line gives the impression of a baseboard in the background, which makes the ball look as if it is sitting on a floor. A small door drawn at the baseboard line changes the scale dramatically and makes the ball seem monumental.

In the foreground the space under the ball could be a table, a floor , or the earth. On the table they may use a pattern for a tablecloth, on the floor they may invent a floor covering and for the earth additions like grass, rocks, and other natural elements may be used. "Bob's Bowl", was Zane Trueblood's solution to this figure/ground problem (p. 67).

Let the students choose from these options for creating space. They may also use the various techniques of charcoal drawing: wet, dry, rubbing, erasing, and layering. The more the students practice and experiment with putting the charcoal on, rubbing it out, adding it back in, and making a wash with compressed charcoal, the better they will become at using charcoal. The drawing may be fixed with Blair no-odor spray fixative or inexpensive hair spray.

Zane Trueblood, Grade 4/5, Charcoal

Michelle Divencenco, Grade 4

GOALS

To experiment with charcoal and increase the students' technical knowledge of the material and its properties. To increase the awareness of how to construct space on a two-dimensional sheet of paper. To improve critical and creative thinking skills.

ART HISTORY REFERENCE

Frank Helmuth Auerbach was exiled to England at the age of 8, and orphaned by Hitler soon afterwards. He entered art school as a teenager in 1948 and has spent his life making paintings and drawings from the posed model or from quick landscape scribbles done outside. He has worked ten hours a day, seven days a week in the same studio in northwest London for over 40 years.

SUMMARY OF STEPS

1. Hand out the Chiaroscuro I drawing.
2. Add a horizontal line halfway from the top.
3. Select background.
4. Compose foreground.
5. Select values for background and foreground
6. Experiment with charcoal techniques
7. Spray Fix

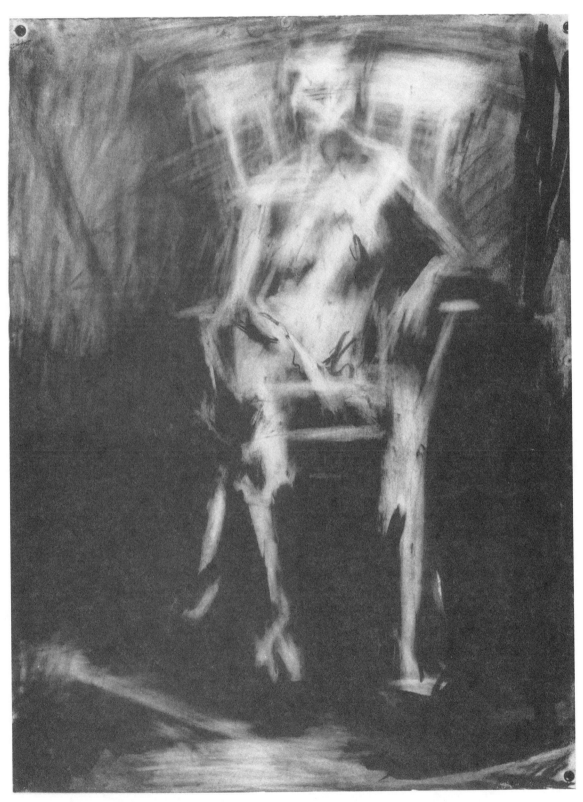

Frank Helmuth Auerbach, British, b. 1913. *Untitled (E.O.W. Nude),* charcoal and pastel with stumping, erasing, scraping, and brushed fixative on white wove paper, 1961, 78 x 57.3 cm. Restricted gift of Mr. and Mrs. Willard Gidwitz, 1993.17. Photograph © 1995, The Art Institute of Chicago. All rights reserved.

REVERSED CHARCOAL: DARK TO LIGHT

BRIEF OVERVIEW

Instead of adding black marks to white paper, the students will work on blackened paper—erasing out the whites and adding blacks. It helps to have done The Overlapping Shapes lesson in Section Three first but it's not mandatory. The other lesson that might precede this one is the Cylinder Study.

If the still life recommended here will not work in your classroom, see Appendix II on still life setups. That can help you decide the best way to set this up in your classroom.

Value change, that is, moving from light to dark, creates a sense of depth and space on a flat piece of paper. Value changes guide the eye around a drawing. With value change we sense we are moving into, out of, and around space. We use a range of grays, from light to dark to interpret light falling on form.

Since we see in color, we don't discriminate value changes as much as we do color changes. This exercise should increase the students' awareness of the importance of light and dark in a drawing.

SUPPLIES

1. 12" x 18" drawing paper
2. Vine charcoal
3. Kneaded eraser
4. Plastic eraser
5. Compressed charcoal

THE SETUP

Set up a still life that sits against a wall. Use a patterned cloth under the still life and a striped cloth behind it—or put a calendar behind it, or an empty picture frame, a hat hanging on a hook, or some other object. This setup helps the students to visualize the background and the foreground.

Set the students up around the still life. Give each student a piece of paper and a piece of vine charcoal. Have the students draw a line around the border of the paper one inch in from the edge to frame what they are looking at.

The students now cover the entire sheet of paper with vine charcoal inside the border. Wipe the charcoal over the paper with medium pressure to avoid as much as possible making charcoal dust. Sometimes two layers lightly one on top of the other, one horizontally and one vertically, can help counter the dust problem. If you have the art kit, use the big chunk of vine charcoal to cover the paper. (A garbage can placed in the middle of the room will give the students a place to shake the dust gently off the paper into the can). Ask the students not to blow the dust off their papers; it will fill and coat the room if blown around.

The students will use the erasers to draw with. Using the plastic eraser, erase the entire shape of the first object. Erase the entire shape of each object one after another in the still life. They will not be able to erase the charcoal entirely. It will leave some texture on the page, but that is one of the qualities of this material and this process.

Drew Cheshire, Grade 4/5, Charcoal

Using the eraser, draw the table line behind the objects. To locate this line, the students should close one eye and look at the objects, noticing where the back edge of the table intersects the objects in their drawings.

The plastic eraser will get dirty during this process. To clean it, simply rub the dirty side on a piece of scratch paper until the black comes off. In Chiaroscuro II there is a section on using erasers.

Ask the students to create the pattern of the table cloth. The kneaded erasers may be used to rub out charcoal or stamp and press out designs or marks. This eraser can be twisted and molded into flat or pointed shapes. Use the kneaded eraser to create the pattern of the drapery and any shapes in the background. Erase the table top, except for the shadows.

As the kneaded eraser gets dirty it will cease functioning. To clean it, stretch it apart like pulling taffy or bubble gum out, and then roll it over on top of itself until there is a clean surface. It is best to try not to pull it completely apart. Stretching cleans

Ben Verhoeven, Grade 6, Reversed Charcoal

it, and then it can be rolled back into any usable shape. If for example, you have grapes in the still life, the students could press the kneaded eraser into the paper and turn and twist it in a circle to create the shapes of grapes.

Use only vine charcoal to start with, but after the shapes and patterns are erased out, use the vine and the compressed charcoal to add the dark side of the form back into the drawing. Use the vine and compressed charcoal to add details and texture to the objects, outline areas that need to be defined, and add more charcoal to areas that need to be darker. The students can follow the rules of the Chiaroscuro lesson and make up the light and dark sides, or you can direct a specific light source. Possible sources might be: sunlight through the windows, turning off the overhead lights or by turning off one bank of overhead lights. A spotlight can be placed on one side of the still life.

Erasers are tools, not toys. Sometimes students are often infatuated with the erasers, and want to play with them.

GOALS

This exercise provides practice in adding and subtracting charcoal. We reverse the thinking process, subtracting light areas instead of adding dark areas. This will be a flat drawing if the dark side is not added back onto the forms. Students increase their technical knowledge and skills in using charcoal.

SUMMARY OF STEPS

1. Set up a still life.
2. Draw a one-inch border around the paper.
3. Fill the entire page with vine charcoal.
4. Erase out all the objects in the still life.
5. Erase out the pattern in the drapery.
6. Erase out the table top.
7. Add the dark side and the shadows back in with the charcoal.
8. Use both erasers.
9. Spray fix.

Joe Vito, Grade 4/5, Reversed Charcoal

Amanda Chiavini, Grade 5, Erased Charcoal

SIMPLE STILL LIFE IN CHARCOAL
Foundation Exercise

BRIEF OVERVIEW

After the students have practiced using charcoal in the Chiaroscuro lesson, this exercise provides the opportunity for them to use the process to interpret a still life. Begin by reminding them of the various ways to use charcoal: rubbing out and adding back in, layering, erasing—all to create value changes. This exercise will need a designated light source. The windows provide a good light source if the classroom has space to set a still life up at the windows, or the overhead lights can be turned off to create shadows.

The still life should be at least four objects sitting on a piece of fabric with one side to the light. The side of the objects closest to the light source, which is the first place the light strikes the forms, will therefore be the light side and will have the hot spot. The other side is then the designated dark side. Remind the students that they are seeing in color and as artists they are interpreting the light into values of black, gray, and white.

Two-dimensional space is dependent on value change. Moving from light to dark in a drawing creates volume and a sense of depth. Really young students (perhaps the third and fourth graders), when they first do a drawing exercise like this, may be able to create only a dark and a light side on the forms. As they do more drawings, their skill with manipulating and creating more than one gray will improve.

The ability to determine value changes depends on the students' level of thinking and reasoning skills because in a sense they are making up the value changes by understanding the process of chiaroscuro. Never force students to follow the instructions precisely; an exercise has as many results as there are students in the room.

It is best to think of instructions as a starting point. They will get the basic techniques and then understand them by doing the exercise. It's better not to have a definite end product in mind.

Value changes on forms are not specific. Artists must understand how light falls on forms and interpret it as they want their drawings perceived. An artist may not actually see each gradation as the light changes across the form, but senses where the light changes and then experiments with different places—rubbing, erasing, and layering until it looks right. The dark on the forms may not look as black as it can be made with the charcoal. These are problems the artist must solve to complete a drawing. The students must make similar choices and experiment with their materials to find out the answers. Every student will have a different experience with the materials, and will use them differently.

Austin Shaw-Phillips, Grade 5, Charcoal

THE SETUP

SUPPLIES

1. Vine charcoal
2. Compressed charcoal
3. 12" x 18" white drawing paper
4. Chamois
5. Kneaded eraser
6. Plastic eraser
7. Rag

Arrange four or five students around a still life. Appendix II will give you options for these arrangements, if the one recommended here won't work in your classroom. Remind the students of the process for using charcoal. Place the still life so that there is a definite light source—a window, a flood light, or perhaps by turning off one bank of overhead lights.

First have the students draw a border around the paper one inch from the edge to prevent them from drawing to the edge of the paper. Begin with the vine charcoal, drawing the outlines of the objects on the paper. They should draw the forms as big as their hands no smaller than their fists. Have them start with the object in the front and add the others onto it. The lesson Overlapping Shapes covers this process of drawing front to back.

They may use the chamois or a tissue to rub off any outline they want to change. Once they have all four objects in outline, they will determine the dark side of every form in the drawing and begin rubbing vine charcoal in that area. They should cover at least a third of the form.

Next, using a finger, a tissue, or a stump, they wipe and rub the charcoal from this first area into the middle area and top of the form, remembering to leave the spot at the top where the light strikes the form first—the hot spot. The hot spot is the whitest area of the drawing. Have them go back into the dark side and add another layer of charcoal. Whenever charcoal is rubbed, the value is lightened.

If they have too much charcoal on the drawing, especially in the lightest areas at the top, have them use the kneaded eraser to lift out the charcoal. To use a kneaded eraser, just press it into the area to be removed and lift it out. You can rub the spot a little, but once the eraser has picked up the charcoal it becomes dirty and unusable; it must be cleaned. To clean it, simply pull the eraser apart like stretching taffy, then roll it back up. Then the students can continue to use the clean sides of the eraser.

The compressed charcoal could be handed out now. It is very black and somewhat richer than vine. It can be put over vine or placed directly on the paper. It can be put on by wiping it off the flat side, the square end, or the corner of the edge where two sides meet.

Pressure is a factor with compressed charcoal. Light pressure will let the texture of the paper show through, which is considered a gray value. Firm pressure creates a very dark black. It is harder to erase compressed charcoal, so hand it out after the students have worked with the vine for a while. It is nice to draw lines with it for pattern or details.

Next establish the shadows under the forms. Pick a value for the table top and the area behind the forms. The rule of thumb is to place a dark value beside a white or gray but not a dark next to a dark area—basically avoid two of the same values side by side. Usually the light areas will appear to come forward and the dark areas will fall back.

No-odor spray fix or hair spray can be used to fix these drawings.

Jon Strowbridge, Grade 4, Charcoal

GOALS

The students should begin to understand how to interpret the way light falls on forms. Using charcoal, they create the illusion of volume and space by manipulating value. Their technical knowledge of both types of charcoal improves as well as their understanding of both kinds of charcoal. This exercise involves decision-making skills and critical thinking.

SUMMARY OF STEPS

1. Set up still life with light source.
2. Draw a border on drawing.
3. Draw objects large.
4. Draw objects from front to back.
5. Use chamois to erase.
6. Identify hot spot and leave white.
7. Add vine to the dark side of form.
8. Rub vine from dark to the gray area.
9. Hand out compressed charcoal.
10. Add shadows.
11. Add details to foreground.
12. Select value for background.
13. Spray fix.
14. Display and discuss the drawings.

Jiri Balcar, Czechoslovakian, 1929–1968, *Four Figures at a Table*, watercolor and pen and black ink, with touches of pen and blue, red and brown ink, and colored wash transfer, on cream wove paper, 1967, 44.9 x 31.2 cm. Mr. and Mrs. Jacques Baruch, gift in honor of Harold Joachim, 1977.59. Photograph © 1995, The Art Institute of Chicago. All rights reserved.

WET CHARCOAL

BRIEF OVERVIEW

This exercise continues to concentrate on value studies. It's a good idea to have done the Chiaroscuro exercise already. This exercise also prepares the students for ink studies. The students will not be using an actual light source in this exercise; they will create a pattern of light and dark that will help them to understand the effects of light and dark in a drawing. They will also learn the process for manipulating compressed charcoal as a wet medium.

This is a slow process, dependent upon constantly returning the brush to the water, then picking up small amounts of black compressed charcoal and moving it as a wash to the gray areas. It offers the opportunity to practice making layers of charcoal.

Sarah Dubrasich, Grade 5, Wax and Wet Charcoal

THE SETUP

Set up a still life with a white cloth or white piece of paper underneath it and a patterned cloth behind it. Use dark objects like black bottles, an eggplant, or a Danish squash. Avoid objects with mirrored or reflective surfaces. Dark matte surfaces absorb light, making it easier for the students to translate the surface qualities to their paper.

Give each student a piece of tag board, a piece of compressed charcoal, a piece of wax, a little water and a brush. Have the students draw a light outline of the shapes in the still life with their vine charcoal. Ask the students to draw the bottles and vegetables large enough to fill three-quarters of the page.

The students start with the piece of wax, pushing it firmly onto the paper, and rubbing it on any area of the drawing they intend to remain light in value. They will need to rub over an area a couple of times, with firm pressure, to get the wax on the paper.

Next take the compressed charcoal and put it on the areas to be dark and one side of the objects. Leave an area between the wax and the black compressed charcoal. Now the drawing has wax areas, black areas, and empty areas.

To get the gray areas, the students will use the brush and water. Wet the brush, squeeze out the excess water, and dip the tip back in the water. Wipe the wet brush into the black charcoal area, it will pick up some black of the charcoal in the bristles. This will create a gray value. Transfer the gray value off the brush into the empty areas, dipping the tip into the water once or twice to continue painting.

The charcoal will stay in the brush quite awhile. The students will continue to get a gray from dipping the brush a couple times after in the water. Each time the wash will be a little lighter. Let the paper dry. Wipe the brush in the charcoal area to create more of the gray wash.

When the brush dries out, it will become hard to manipulate. The tip of the brush will fold over when it needs more water, or it will bush out. At that point, dip the brush back in the water. If the students just dip the tip of the brush in the water, they won't have problems with the paper rippling because it's too wet, and they can control the effect of the gray value they are creating with a wet brush in the charcoal.

The first black areas that were washed over will dry a medium gray value. When they are dry, use the compressed charcoal again on top to darken the area further.

Use a couple of light washes over the wax areas. The students may want to try to put charcoal directly on the wax lightly and then wash over that area.

In the end, the students should have a wax resist side with a wash on it, a medium gray area, and a black side to each object. Treat the foreground and background areas also by making choices between wax, charcoal, wash, and the white of the paper. The students should add the shadows under the forms and the pattern on the cloth in the background with their tools to create these spaces and patterns.

SUPPLIES

1. 12" x 18" tag board, 150 lb

2. Compressed vine charcoal

3. Watercolor brush

4. Water in cup

5. Wax (paraffin, white candle)

Austin Shaw-Phillips, Grade 5, Wet Charcoal

GOALS

To see the effects of light and dark on the space in a drawing. To practice another technique with charcoal. Decision-making skills, hand-eye coordination, and planning are increased by this exercise.

SUMMARY OF STEPS

1. Draw the shapes.
2. Rub wax on light areas.
3. Wipe charcoal on dark areas.
4. Leave area between wax and charcoal.
5. Use a wet brush, wash into charcoal.
6. Put wash over wax once or twice.
7. Put the gray wash in the empty space.
8. Compose the pattern of the drapery.
9. Choose values for background.
10. Choose values for foreground.
11. Add shadows under forms.

Brooke Cutsforth, College Student, Drawing I, Cross-hatched Still Life

CROSS-HATCHING PRACTICE
Foundation Exercise

BRIEF OVERVIEW

Crosshatching is one of the techniques used in pencil drawing to create value. The hatching marks or stroke should be made close together and as ordered as possible. The hatching strokes may go horizontally, vertically, or diagonally. There may be single sets of hatching marks or the strokes may be overlapped.

The more times an area is covered with hatching strokes, the darker the area becomes. To make a cross-hatch, the strokes are stacked on top of each other; one set goes on the diagonal to the right and then switches to a diagonal to the left; one set is horizontal and one is vertical. The pressure put on the pencil and which number of pencil lead is used will also affect the lightness and darkness of the value. Heavy pressure makes dark areas; light pressure makes light areas.

Pencil leads come in light and dark leads. The F lead is in the middle with the soft B leads moving from HB to 6B—each level gets softer and darker as the number increases. Anything beyond 6B is too soft; and too difficult to sharpen to use. On the other side of the scale the pencil leads starting with H get harder and lighter as the numbers increase. A 6H lead is very, very light and very hard. This side of the spectrum is used by architects for drafting when working on thin paper.

THE SETUP

On a piece of scratch paper ask the students to try the HB, 3B and the 6B pencils one at a time. Using the tip of the pencil make diagonal, horizontal, and vertical hatched areas with each pencil, changing the pressure from light for one set of marks to medium for some and firm for some. In this way the students can see the difference between the leads. HB should be lighter than 6B.

Using the ellipse structure from the cylinder study, have the students design a vase or bottle. If they haven't done the cylinder exercise, this makes no sense so just have them draw an imaginary object. Then practice placing hatching on the object or vase.

Start with the HB pencil and hatch the entire form lightly in one direction. Then take the 3B pencil and hatch two-thirds of the form, leaving a section of the HB pencil (a third is good). Finally, use the 6B pencil on the last third of the form. This should result in the forms being one-third light, one-third medium gray, and one third dark. Experiment with the light and dark pencil leads and light and heavy pressure on the pencil.

The pencils may be used alone. An HB could be layered over itself to create various levels or degrees of light values. When the 6B pencil is layered, different degrees of dark values develop. The advantage of this difference is the HB can be used for value changes on a form that is entirely in the light and the 6B pencil can be used to show value change on a form that sits mostly in shadow or further away from the light. Try to keep hatching strokes close together; if they are too far apart they will appear more like a cobweb than a value change. Practice making a rhythmic stroke.

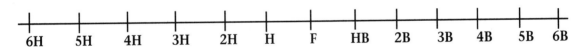

| 6H | 5H | 4H | 3H | 2H | H | F | HB | 2B | 3B | 4B | 5B | 6B |

SUPPLIES

1. HB, 3B, 6B pencils
2. White drawing paper
3. Tissues

SUMMARY OF STEPS

1. Try one pencil at a time.
2. Use tip to make hatching strokes.
3. Hatch vertically, horizontally, diagonally.
4. Note light and dark leads.
5. Draw a cylinder.
6. Hatch with HB on entire form.
7. Hatch with 3B on two-thirds of form.
8. Hatch with 6B on final third of form.
9. Keep hatching strokes close together.
10. Reinforce gray and dark areas.

GOALS

To increase the students technical knowledge and skill level in using cross hatching. To improve the student's coordination in making hatching marks. To understand the difference in pencil leads. To develop an understanding of various approaches to creating value changes through choice of pencil leads and pressures.

Giorgio Morandi, *Vase with Flowers*, 1924, etching, 9 1/4" x 7 3/4". The San Francisco Museum of Modern Art. Gift of Helen Crocker Russell Memorial Fund, 72.29.

CROSS-HATCHING A STILL LIFE: Creating Value

BRIEF OVERVIEW

Before doing this exercise the students should do the Cylinder Study in Section One, Chiaroscuro I Section Two, and Overlapping Shapes in Section Three. Set up a still life of bottles on a table with a white cloth or paper underneath. Use short and tall bottles, and try to have the students sit no more than four to five feet away from at least three bottles. If a series of small still life setups for five to six students is not possible, form the students' desks in a big circle around one long table in the middle. The bottles can be grouped in sections of four or five up and down the table. This last arrangement probably needs a minimum of 12 to 18 bottles.

To help the students see value changes, use white bottles and black bottles. Bottles can be spray-painted black or white. Avoid reflective surfaces, which can be confusing.

THE SETUP

Ask the students to draw and arrange on their papers any four bottles they can see. Remind them to use the ellipse to form the top and bottom of these bottles. After they form the opening at the top, they can use the half ellipse down the bottle to build the rest of the cylinder or bottle form.

Next discuss the rule of perspective for showing objects moving back in space. As objects move back in space they move up the paper. Each base is placed higher up the paper from the first and most frontal object. Remind them also that overlapping shapes will create a sense of space on the paper. With this information, the students can construct and compose their drawing.

After they have the outlines of the bottles drawn, using the HB pencil, very lightly hatch every form, the background, and the foreground. Cover the entire paper lightly with a diagonal hatching stroke. The have created the lightest value in the drawing.

Now the students decide from what side the light is falling on their forms. Leave the light side with the first layer of HB pencil strokes. Then using the 3B pencil with medium-to-light pressure, hatch over the areas to be gray and black. The first hatching strokes were diagonal, use a vertical or horizontal stroke for the second section of hatching. Be sure to leave light areas of HB hatching strokes.

SUPPLIES

1. 12" x 18" white drawing paper
2. HB, 3B, 6B pencils
3. Pencil sharpener

Next, take the 6B pencil and hatch vertically and then diagonally over the darkest areas of the drawing. Remember to hatch the shadows, and the dark areas of the background as well as the dark side of the objects. In the dark areas, the students can hatch the area three or four times to create a strong dark.

Select the pencil needed to go back into the drawing and reinforce any area not dark enough or medium gray enough. The final hatching strokes should follow the object's shape around. Horizontal strokes tend to finish the surface of bowls and bottles.

SUMMARY OF STEPS

1. Review Chiaroscuro I.
2. Review Cylinder Study to draw four bottles.
3. Review Overlapping Shapes to compose drawing.
4. Hatch the entire drawing with the HB pencil.
5. Start with light pressure on the light area.
6. Use medium pressure on gray area.
7. Hatch the medium to dark areas with the 3B.
8. Use firm pressure in dark areas.
9. Hatch all dark areas on forms and grounds with 6B.
10. Reuse the HB,3B,6B to reinforce weak areas.
11. Remember to hatch back and foreground.

GOALS

To understand how to build value with overlapping strokes, changing pencil leads and changing pressure on the pencil. To test the students' ability to plan a still life with the rules of perspective. Students improve hand-eye coordination and use critical thinking skills that involve personal decision making.

Kathleen Eide, Grade 4, Still Life

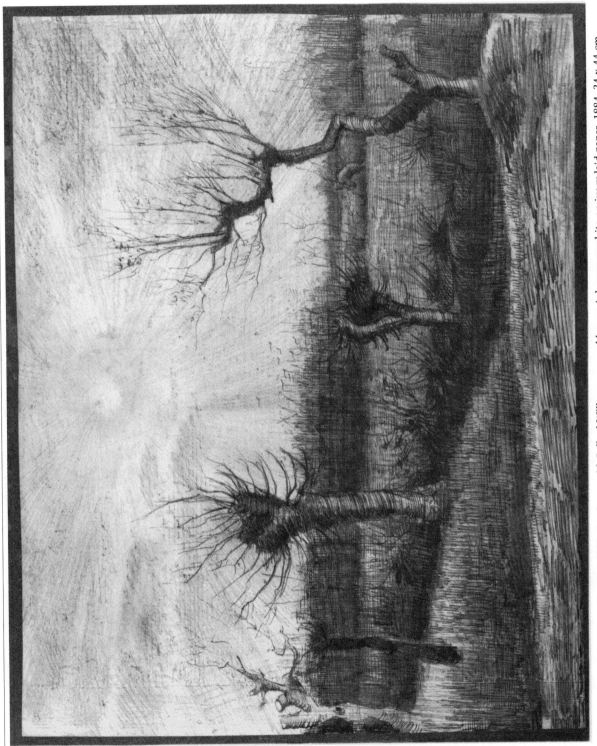

Vincent van Gogh, Dutch, 1853-1890, *Landscape with Pollard Willows*, pen and brown ink over graphite on ivory laid paper, 1884, 34 x 44 cm. Robert Allerton Fund, 1969.268. Photograph © 1995, The Art Institute of Chicago. All rights reserved.

"It probably got in through the window."

William T. Wiley, *It Probably Got in Through the Window*, 1965, pencil drawing, 14" x 18" (35.5 x 45.7 cm). The San Francisco Museum of Modern Art. Gift of Dr. and Mrs. Willam R. Fielder, 86.125.

PENCIL STILL LIFE: Rubbed and Erased

SUPPLIES

1. HB, 6B pencils
2. 12" x 18" tag board
3. Plastic eraser
4. Tissues
5. Pencil sharpener

A BRIEF OVERVIEW

This exercise should be preceded by the Cylinder study in Section One, Overlapping Shapes in Section Three, and Chiaroscuro I in Section Two. Value change is achieved by rubbing and erasing in this exercise.

THE SETUP

Arrange the students in front of a still life. Appendix II will give you still life setup options for your classroom. Give each student the supplies.

Have the students draw a border around the edge of the paper one inch in from the edge. The students have now constructed a frame, a window of sorts to look through at the objects, instead of thinking of the paper as flat. They should think of the border as a picture frame surrounding the objects they are drawing. Sometimes it helps the students to hold the paper up between themselves and the still life. Placing it at arm's length, in front of themselves, and just below eye level, they pretend to look through the paper framing what they will draw. Keeping the paper below eye level they can see over the top and then judge the number of objects that will fit on their paper. Doing this exercise helps the students to visualize and translate real space into two-dimensional space.

The rules for constructing a still life on the paper can be found in the Overlapping Shapes and Cylinder lessons. The forms in the drawing should be drawn as large as their hands and not smaller than their fists.

Andrew Swanson, Grade 4,
Erased Pencil Still Life

The students select and draw three or four objects on their papers. In the Chiaroscuro I lesson, they practiced creating light and dark on an object, simulating the way light falls on form. Remind them of that lesson, as they will follow the same procedures now, using pencils instead of charcoal.

The students need a light source. Turning off one bank of overhead lights will work and put the objects half in light and half in dark, or set the still life up by the windows and use a natural light source on one side of the still life.

Start with the 6B pencil and have the students hatch the darkest side of the objects, which will be the side of the objects furthest from the light source. They will work from the dark side to the light side. After they have darkened a third to a half of the surface on all their objects in the drawing, have them take the tissue and rub into the hatched area, moving the pencil lead that the tissue picks up over the rest of **the entire drawing.** This creates a warm gray.

Using the plastic eraser, erase out the lightest side on the objects. They should hatch over the foreground and the background also, starting with the darkest area. Then rub the lead over the lightest areas. Leave some of the gray rubbed area for the middle value. A good formula might be to darken one-third, rub and leave one-third, erase one-third of every form. Light will sometimes fall in lines down and through the gray or dark areas; students may want to erase small light lines as well as the major areas with the eraser.

If an area is erased too much, rub over it again with the tissue after picking up some lead in a dark area. Try erasing light out of the 6B areas also.

If the area in shadow was rubbed out too much, take the 6B pencil and go over the darkest area again. Remember to add the shadows and the table line behind the objects, along with something in the background. The background may be just value changes, the window, or a plant across the room.

SUMMARY OF STEPS

1. Draw a border on the paper.
2. Think of the paper as a window.
3. Frame still life with this window.
4. Plan what objects to draw.
5. Draw forms large.
6. Establish the light source.
7. Hatch the dark side of the form.
8. Rub the lead over all the drawing.
9. Erase the light areas.
10. Repeat process in background and foreground.

GOALS

Students can compare pencil with charcoal and examine the differences between the two materials in creating value changes. This helps students understand the difference between materials. This exercise gives students visual experience in interpreting three-dimensional space into two-dimensional space. It improves hand-eye coordination. Students must calculate, plan, and process visual information.

In this exercise, the drawing is approached as a whole—not one part to another part. The important understanding is the relationship between the objects and the space.

Nate Ketel, Grade 5, Pencil Still Life

Richard Diebenkorn, *Untitled*, watercolor, gouache and pencil, ca. 1946, 11" x 13 1/2". San Francisco Museum of Modern Art. Gift of Jermayne MacAgy, 55.6939.

WARM-UP FOR INK DRAWING
Foundation Exercise

BRIEF OVERVIEW

Working with ink takes patience and planning. In ink drawing, the student builds layers, working from light to dark. Part of each layer should be left when adding a second or third wash. The goal is to keep a section of each layer showing in the drawing. This exercise allows the students to practice the process of ink drawing and improve their skills.

A quill brush is used on its tip only. The students should not scrub with the brush. Once the brush runs out of water or ink, it gets bushy, and looks electrified. It must be dipped back into the water and brought back to a point. Students should be reminded that a brush is not like a ball-point pen, with ever-flowing ink. Part of ink drawing is the continual dipping of the brush back into the water and the ink.

Ina Song Drawing with Ink, Grade 4

THE SETUP

SUPPLIES

1. Tag board, 12" x 18"
2. Quill or watercolor brush
3. Sumi ink or India ink
4. Water
5. Three small jars
6. Rags or paper towels

Each student will need three small containers—one with a half cup of water, one with a dilute mixture of ink and water, and one with straight Sumi ink in it. This setup may also be shared by two students.

For the dilute mixture, place 1/4 cup of water in a small jar or dish and dip the tip of the brush into the ink. Transfer that small amount of ink on the brush to the 1/4 cup of water and mix together. This is the first gray wash. They may need only a drop of ink for this first mixture. If it's too light add one more drop of ink to get a light gray.

On the tag board, each student draws a few shapes—a circle, an ellipse, an oval, a worm shape, or whatever organic shape they can think of. Geometric shapes are harder to deal with, so start with the circle family of shapes.

If they have done the Chiaroscuro I exercise, they should have an easy time with this one. Leave the hot spot, or spot where light first strikes the form, the white of the paper. Using the gray wash mixture, cover the rest of the entire form with this first gray wash. Cover all four or five forms in the same way. Let the forms dry.

If the students get too much water in the brush, it will drip and be hard to control. Having a few paper towels close by provides a good place to blot out excess water or wash.

Use a half cup of water to rinse out the brush between washes, at the end of a cycle, or during a wash to bring the brush back to a tip.

Take the first ink wash and add a small amount of ink to mix a second wash. To make the second wash, dip the very end of the brush into the ink and then transfer that to the first wash water. By now the first washes are probably dry on the paper. Leaving one-quarter of the first wash on all the forms, cover the remaining three-quarters of the form with the second wash.

Make a third wash by adding a little more ink to the wash mixture. Leave half of the form in the first two washes. Cover the bottom half or dark side of the form with the third wash.

Dip the damp—but not too wet—brush into the full-strength Sumi or India ink and wash over the bottom quarter of each form. Let it dry. Using straight ink, add a shadow to the bottom of each form.

GOALS

This exercise develops the students' hand-eye coordination. In addition they are learning a new technique. The students develop a basic technical knowledge of the ink drawing process. This exercise takes patience and careful handling of materials. India ink is permanent. It also requires thinking and planning in order to keep the various degrees of gray in the drawing that result from leaving some of each layer.

SUMMARY OF STEPS

1. Draw a few organic shapes.
2. Mix the first wash.
3. Leave the hot spot.
4. Wash over the rest of the form.
5. Let it dry.
6. Mix the second wash.
7. Put the second wash over three-fourths of the form.
8. Let each layer dry.
9. Make a third wash.
10. Put the third wash on half of the form.
11. Use full strength ink on last quarter.
12. Add a shadow in ink.

Amanda Chiavini, Grade 5, Ink and Wash Drawing

BUILDING INK WASHES

BRIEF OVERVIEW

Sumi or India ink is permanent; point this out to the students and remind them to be as careful as possible. In ink drawing, the white of the paper is the lightest value. There is no way to erase or add white short of taking a razor blade and scraping off the ink, so the areas to be white must be left untouched.

The exercise, Warm Up for Ink Drawing, will tell you how to make the ink washes. The Chiaroscuro lesson also is valuable in preparing the students to judge the location of the value changes. The hot spot should be left the white of the paper.

In ink drawing, the ink washes dry lighter than they look when they are applied. Each time the students wash over an area it will darken just a little more. We tend to think of ink as being only black. Adding water lightens the value of the ink wash, and layering ink makes different grays. Continuing to add water to ink lightens the value; adding more ink darkens the value. There is a range from light gray, through medium gray, to dark gray, and they are all distinguishable from the black of straight ink.

The artist can make many degrees of dark by continuing to add a drop of ink to the wash water. Let each wash dry before adding another wash over it. Always leave some of the previous wash. In ink, you work from light to dark.

Ink drawing takes patience. The brush will run out of wash and will have to be dipped back in the wash regularly. The brush is not a shovel; the students cannot scoop up enough material to last through the entire drawing. Rather, the process is one of washing over one small area at a time, looking at it, and then dipping the brush in the wash and continuing.

Each wash *must* dry before the next one can be added over or on it. Wet wash on wet wash will run and dry as one mottled value. Too much water on the paper will shred it or warp it.

THE SETUP

Arrange a still life of white objects for the students to study. Select a light source; turn off one bank of overhead lights or sit the still life near the window.

Have the students use the HB pencil to *lightly* sketch the shape of the objects. Ask them to note with a light line where they think the light changes occur on the objects. Divide the lightest side where it turns to light gray, then divide where the light seems to be a medium gray, and finally draw a line where the darkest side begins. Ask the students to make only four breaks. The students should draw the forms as big as their hands—no smaller than their fists. The Cylinder Study and Overlapping Shapes exercises are helpful before doing this one.

Discuss the direction of the light source and determine the location of the hot spot on the forms in the still life. The students are to leave the white of the paper for the hot spot.

SUPPLIES

1. 12" x 18" tag board
2. Quill or watercolor brush
3. HB pencil
4. Three small containers
5. Water
6. India ink or Sumi ink
7. Rag or paper towels for spills
8. Wax or paraffin

Ask the students to consider where to use the wax. Any area that needs a textured surface, or any space they want to remain white with black around, it may be covered with wax. Remember to rub the wax *firmly* into the paper.

As in the ink practice, mix the first gray wash with a little ink and water. Then use the wash throughout the entire drawing on every form; cover the foreground and the background areas, including the wax areas. Leave all white areas untouched. Don't use too much water; work off the tip of the brush, constantly dipping the brush in the wash. Wipe the brush on the rag or paper towels to blot excess water. Clean water should be available to rinse out the brush between wash layers. Let each layer dry.

Amanda Carey, Grade 4, Ink Washes

Sarah Fennell, Grade 5, Ink Wash with Wax

Follow the division lines and use the second wash on the gray area. The second wash will increase the darkness of the value on the object. Leave the white, leave part of the first wash, and put the second wash on everything but the lightest areas and the hot spot. If they want large light areas in some places in the foreground and background, they might leave more of the first wash showing or leave the white of the paper. Let it dry.

The third wash again increases the dark value. Mix a third wash and put it on the forms, from the divisions for medium dark to the darkest areas, including the background and the shadows under the objects. Let it dry.

At one point they may want to keep either the second or third wash and get another jar to mix the next wash so they can work between these two washes. If an area dries too light, use another layer of the second or the third wash to darken it just a little more.

They can continue mixing washes by adding a little ink to their water and washing over areas of the drawing as long as there is time and interest.

To finish, use the ink straight, placing it on the darkest areas of the drawing. Have the students leave parts of their previous washes, but if they want, they can put stripes of black ink on the gray wash areas—or dots or any mark they can invent to indicate pattern, light, or direction.

SUMMARY OF STEPS

1. Identify a light source.
2. Make a light outline of the forms.
3. Map out value changes on forms.
4. Leave white of the paper for hot spot.
5. Firmly rub the wax on gray areas and textured surfaces.
6. Mix first ink wash.
7. The first wash goes on all forms.
8. Put wash on the background and foreground.
9. Let each wash dry.
10. Mix second wash to cover medium to dark gray areas.
11. Leave some of each wash showing.
12. Mix third wash darken more areas.
13. Mix as many washes as needed.
14. Add black to dark side and shadows.

GOALS

This exercise helps students begin to understand the range of gray values available to them. It develops patience and concentration. Each step must be planned, or the drawing will lose a sense of space and depth. Without a value change on the forms, they will appear flat. The students will learn by doing, and they will learn by watching their neighbors' progress. There's no erasing, so all decisions are made on how to move forward. Critical thinking and their decision-making abilities are enhanced.

INK LINE DRAWING

THE SETUP

Select a subject to draw. If the class has a pet hamster, rabbit, chicken or duck, they are fun to try. Perhaps a student could bring the family dog to school one day. A bicycle, or a large form of some kind, is good to try. Place the students in front of the subject. If they fit around the subject better sitting on the floor, use the drawing boards on their laps under their papers.

Dip the tip of the pens in the jar of ink and practice a few strokes on a scrap of paper. This gets the ink flowing through the pen. Pens often have wax on their tips to protect them in shipping; if so run them under hot water before you use them.

The line is blotchy—often thick and sometimes thin. The pen will run out of ink, so the students will work on forming the subject by drawing it one section at a time. Have the students follow the contour of the subject around the perimeter—moving the line in and out.

Use thick lines in the dark or heavy areas and thin lines in light, thin, and airy sections. Ask the students to think about what kind of line to use.

If they place a line somewhere they don't want a line to be, let it dry. Then draw the line where it should go and let that first line remain part of the composition. It may be possible at the end of the drawing to incorporate the unwanted line into the background—but there is no erasing.

SUPPLIES

1. 12" x 18" tag board
2. Speedball pen and point
3. Sumi ink
4. Desk top or drawing board
5. Paper towels

Pierre Bonnard, French, 1867-1947, *Rooster*, brush and black ink, on cream wove paper, 1888—1947, 49.9 x 31.9 cm. Bequest of William McCormick Blair, 1982.1826. Photograph © 1995 The Art Institute of Chicago. All rights reserved.

The pen must be continually dipped back in the ink and wiped off on the side of the jar. Too much ink in the pen will make large blotches. The pen can be turned to the side and tapped a bit when they think it is out of ink and often there will be just a little more to make a fine line with. Do not shake or flip the pens as that will spray ink on others.

GOALS

To practice line drawing and develop decision-making skills. Students must determine the quality of line needed to render the object they are drawing. They must be patient and build the drawing one step at a time because of the limitation of their materials.

Travis McClanahan, Grade 4, Ink Line Drawing

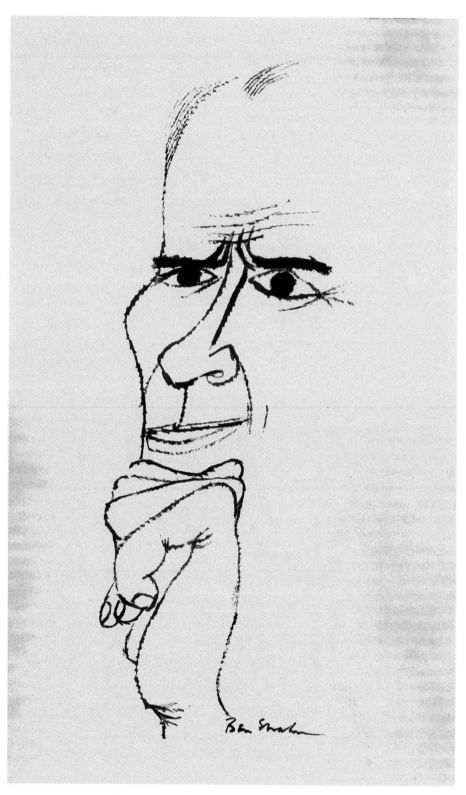

Ben Shahn, American, 1898—1969, *Monroe Wheeler*, brush and black ink on white wove paper, 1918—1969, 49.1 x 32.4 cm. Gift of Monroe Wheeler, 1979.134. Photograph © 1995, The Art Institute of Chicago. All rights reserved.

SECTION THREE:
Perspective

PERSPECTIVE I
Foundation Exercise

BRIEF OVERVIEW

To create the illusion of receding space on a piece of paper a series of steps was developed during the Renaissance. Before you give the steps to the students, this short exercise may help them to understand how and why these directions work.

Visual artists tend to depend on their hand-eye coordination to draw straight lines because these lines have more character and a finer quality than lines drawn with rulers. Beginning students, however, should be allowed to use rulers until their skills with lines improve.

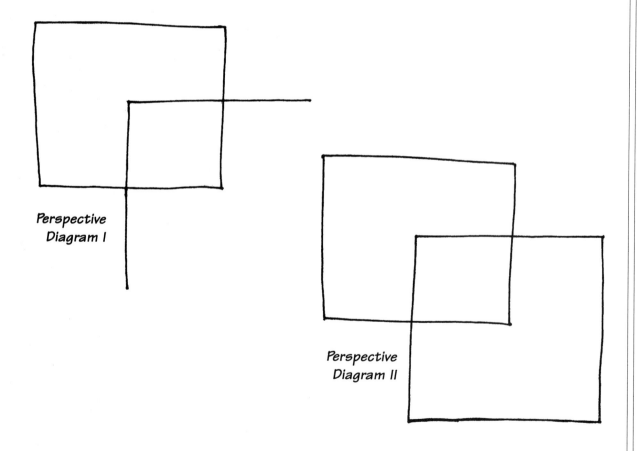

*Perspective
Diagram I*

*Perspective
Diagram II*

THE SETUP

Ask the students to draw a square two inches on a side, with a second square overlapping the bottom right corner of the first square. The second square should be the same size as the first square. To draw the second square, measure one inch down the right vertical line, and make a mark. Then measure one inch across the bottom line of the first box and mark that measurement on the line (Diagrams I, II).

To construct the second box, place the ruler horizontally on the one-inch mark across the vertical side and mark off one inch to either side of the mark, then draw a line through the measurement mark. This two-inch line is the top line of the second box. Place the ruler vertically on the mark on the bottom line of the first box and draw a vertical line connecting it to the horizontal line at the top. Then extend this line down one inch past the mark. Place the ruler vertically on the right end of the top, horizontal line, and draw a two-inch vertical line. Connect the bottom points with a horizontal line.

Using diagonal lines connect the two squares by drawing from the front box to the back box; connect the top left corner of the front box to the back top left corner. Then connect the top right corners with a diagonal line. Using a diagonal line connect the bottom corners, left bottom to back left and right front to back right corner (Diagrams III, IV). They have now made a three-dimensional form. It is no longer two squares it's a cube.

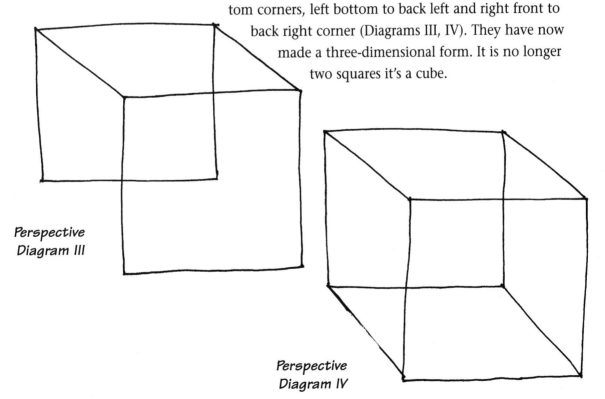

*Perspective
Diagram III*

*Perspective
Diagram IV*

107

This exercise is the first step in understanding how perspective works. Converging diagonal lines are used to indicate space receding. As things get further away from us they also seem to get smaller. To explore this second aspect of perspective ask the students to draw a small box on the paper. Then place a second larger square over the bottom right corner of the first box. Use diagonal lines to connect the top corners from the front to the back box and then connect the bottom corners. The students can see that the box appears to be receding into space.

Have the students practice making boxes by drawing to the left side as well. They can also use the rectangle, or any geometric shape they may want to invent as long as they make two shapes the same and overlap them on one side. To connect any two geometric shapes, a point on the front shape must be connected to the same corner on the matching back shape; both shapes must be the same except for their size. One can be smaller than the other.

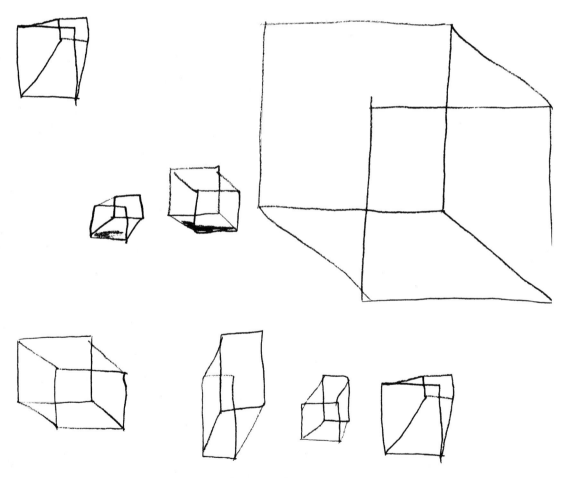

Austin Shaw-Phillips, Grade 5, Perspective Step One

THE VANISHING POINT AND THE HORIZON

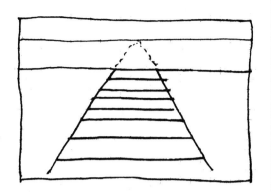

To draw in perspective all diagonal lines will vanish to a point on the horizon. The VP (vanishing point) is located at the point where the diagonal lines receding to the horizon converge. There may be many vanishing points along the horizon in any given drawing as each object may have a different VP.

Give the students a new sheet of paper. Have the students draw a horizon line one-third of the way down the paper from the top. On the bottom third of the paper draw a small square and then draw a larger one over the smaller one's bottom right corner just as they did in the first exercise. Connect the top and bottom corners of the squares. Using a ruler extend the top diagonal lines to the horizon. In addition extend the lines from the bottom corner of the box to the horizon.

Notice that as the lines recede they get closer together, and all the lines are angled in the same direction. In one-point perspective all lines vanish from front to back to one point somewhere out in space. It isn't necessary to actually have a vanishing point on the paper as long as the lines taper together as they move back in space.

To practice one-point perspective have the students draw two receding lines five inches apart vanishing to one point on the horizon from the bottom of the paper. Then ask them to place horizontal lines between the lines. Space the first two horizontal lines one inch apart from the bottom of the paper. Then place each following horizontal line a little closer to the one before it.

To achieve a sense of perspective in drawing, make things smaller and closer together the further away they are. Reduce the space between areas, and use overlapping shapes.

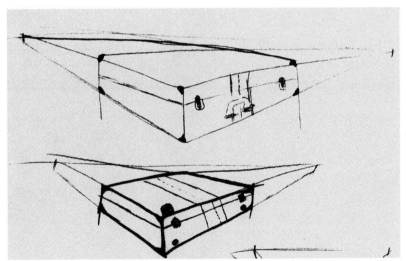

Amanda Chiavini, Grade 5, Two-point Perspective

GOALS

To introduce students to perspective drawing. Concepts in drawing are easier to understand when students experience and use them. In the arts you learn from doing.

*One-point Perspective Landscape
Anna Benedict, Grade 4*

SUMMARY OF STEPS

1. Draw a 2" square.
2. Mark off 1" down one side and across the bottom.
3. Draw a 2" square in the marked-off area.
4. Connect the same top corner of each box from front to back.
5. Connect the same bottom corner of each box from front to back.
6. Exercise #2, draw a small box.
7. Overlap a larger box on one corner.
8. Connect the corners of the boxes front to back.
9. Extend all diagonal lines to horizon.
10. Practice making geometric forms.
11. Start a new paper.
12. Draw a horizon line near top.
13. Draw 2 lines from the bottom of the paper to a VP on the horizon.
14. Draw horizontal lines in between above lines.

*Caleb Ruecker,
Grade 4,
Drawing*

Christo Vladimirov Javacheff, American, b. 1935, *Running Fence, Sonoma and Marin Counties. California*, collage, 1976, Society for Contemporary Art, gift, 1977.116. Photograph © 1995, the Art Institute of Chicago. All rights reserved.

Richard Diebenkorn, *#10 from 41 Etchings,* 1965, drypoint, plate 11" x 6 3/4". San Francisco Museum of Modern Art. William L. Gerstle Collection, 66.7.10. William L. Gerstle Fund Purchase.

OVERLAPPING SHAPES: The First Step in Understanding Perspective
Foundation Exercise

BRIEF OVERVIEW

In this exercise the students study the spatial relationships between the objects in a still life. They should take time observing the placement and the proportions of the objects. In art when people refer to "seeing," they are referring to fine-tuned skills of observation. The Cylinder Study in Section One is helpful to do prior to this one as it teaches students how to draw individual forms.

In pre-Renaissance perspective there were no overlapping shapes. The people and the objects were placed side by side on the same horizontal base line. The important figures were drawn on the bottom row. People or things of lesser importance were drawn toward the top and made smaller. The narrative or story was arranged in bands from the bottom to the top, so people reading the narrative read across and then up. This way of drawing creates a flat space. The Egyptian wall paintings are a good example of early flat art. They show the figures drawn from a side view but the eyes looking forward not sideways. You may want to try a drawing with the students in which they use this horizontal band drawing to tell a story. Then when you introduce Renaissance perspective they will have something to compare it with.

The artists of the Renaissance realized that overlapping shapes created a sense of space and depth in a drawing. By placing one form behind another the artist can translate three-dimensional space on to the flat two dimensional space of the paper. As the objects move back in space, they move from the bottom of the paper to the top. Therefore, the base of each object, moving back in space, is placed one behind the other up the page. The front of the table is the space at the bottom of the drawing paper and the back of the table is the space closer to the top of the page.

You can demonstrate this paper to table relationship with a china marker and a piece of clear Plexiglas. Hold the Plexiglas in front of a still life and, keeping your head in one place, draw the objects where you see them through the Plexiglas. Draw the location of the top and the bottom of each form as accurately as possible.

To draw, the students should be arranged around a table with a still life setup. Each student should be able to see six to eight objects that are placed from the front of the table to the back. Objects that are easiest to draw are eggplants, oranges, grapefruits, vases, bottles, cookie jars, onions, and things without handles or spouts. If you want to include handles do the exercise in the Cylinder lesson first.

THE SETUP

Arrange the students in a semicircle around a table with a still life of different sizes of objects. Try to keep their sitting position approximately four feet from the setup. By sitting at this distance the students have a better view of the objects making it easier for them to fill the page. If they are too far away they tend to miniaturize the objects and lose sense of the proper proportions.

Have the students draw a border about one inch from the edge of the paper. A border around the paper frames the drawing and prevents them from starting the drawing on the edge of the paper. The students should always start their drawings one to two inches away from the paper's edge.

Planning the drawing is very important, so before the students start, go around the room and ask the students what objects they have decided to draw. Have them point to everything they plan to draw. They might, for example, point to an orange and a pitcher, backed by a compote with grapes and a little sugar bowl off to the left in the back. First they should consider which side of the paper they will start on and then on which side of the paper they will place the remaining objects. Ask them to point at where they will start and which way they will draw across the paper. This physical gesturing helps them to plan the drawing and visualize the relationship of real space to paper space.

The drawing is constructed from the front to the back of the paper. They start with the object on the table that is in front of all the others. Using the HB pencil the students should draw lightly, with light pressure on their pencils. If the other objects are to the left of this first object then the students should leave room on the left of the paper; if the other objects are to the right of the first object, they will leave room on the right of the paper. A review of ways to use pencils, marks, and pressure can be found in the warm-up exercise in Section One.

The students will start the drawing near the bottom above their border line with the object in the front of their field of objects. Have them draw each object large (as big as their hands, no smaller than their fists). To draw the second object, look at the objects' base. Have the students take

SUPPLIES

1. 12" x 18" white drawing paper 60 to 80 lb

2. HB, 3B, and 6B drawing pencils

3. White plastic eraser

4. Pencil sharpener

Overlapping Diagram I

Overlapping Diagram II

114

their pencils and, holding them horizontally in front of themselves, line up the base of object 2 with object 1, making a little mark where the base of object 2 seems to intersect on the side of the first object.

Next look at the height of the second object. Is it twice as tall as the first object, a third as tall? Make a mark on the paper to show how tall the object should be compared with the first object. Now draw the object into the space marked off, fitting it behind object 1. Look for a third object and find the base in terms of what is already drawn, find the height and add object 3. Repeat to fill the page.

Overlapping Diagram III

Don't give the students an eraser until they have drawn all the objects on the page, because what they think is a "wrong" line is actually a good line; it shows the students where they do not want the line and from that point they can redraw the line where they do want to place it. If they erase the "wrong" line they have no reference point to work from to draw the correct line—correct only in terms of what students think, not in terms of any reality for correct lines.

Fill the page with objects from all over the table. Look for the back edge of the table and add a line behind the objects where it

Grade 4/5, Glencoe School, Portland, Oregon Overlapping Shapes

intersects the objects for the table.

To darken the shapes they may use their 3B and 6B pencils. The 6B should be used on areas they want to be dark and the 3B should be used in areas to be left lighter.

Grade 4/5, Glencoe School, Portland, Oregon, Overlapping Shapes

INK OPTION

After the students have practiced overlapping shapes, use pen and ink instead of using the pencils. Have them draw the shapes with the pen. Pen and ink is challenging because they cannot erase and because they can vary the quality of the line from thick to thin. Any lines that are bothersome should be washed over with a wet brush and they will become part of the background or the surface of the form, depending on where they were left.

GOALS

The students develop critical thinking skills in judging distance and deciding placement in interpreting the space of the still life to the space of the two-dimensional paper. They must plan out the space and think ahead. Their hand-eye coordination is greatly improved by the calculations they make.

SUMMARY OF STEPS

1. Sit 4 feet from the still life.
2. Draw a border around the paper.
3. Start the drawing near the bottom border.
4. The first object drawn is in front of all others.
5. Locate the base of the second object up the page.
6. Mark off the base and height of the second object.
7. Add the outline of the second object.
8. Repeat base and height measurements for third and fourth objects.
9. Draw objects to fill the page.

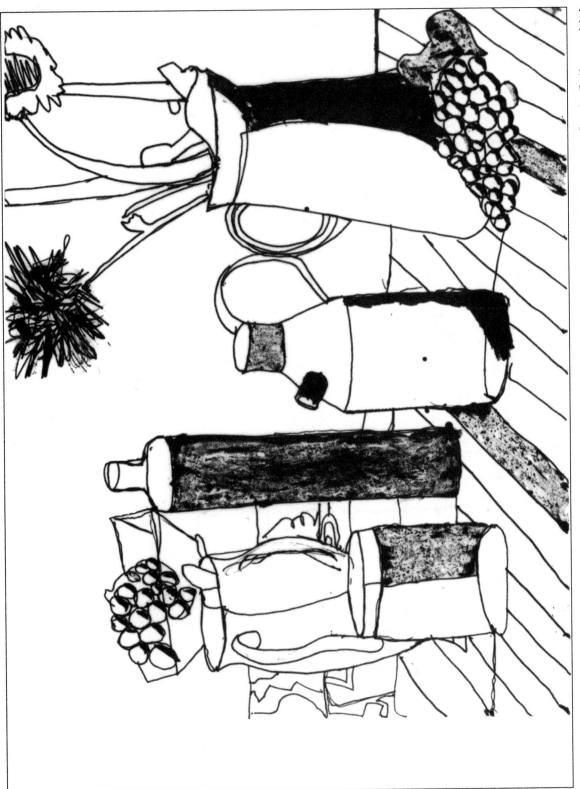

Amanda Chiavini, Grade 5, One-point Perspective

ONE-POINT PERSPECTIVE
Foundation Exercise

BRIEF OVERVIEW

Perspective drawing was the invention of Filippo Brunelleschi, who in 1419 built a colonnade as part of the Foundling Hospital in Florence. The colonnade was designed by repeating a single unit to create a long walkway of arches. He realized that each unit—which he knew to be the same size—appeared to get smaller toward the end. He also noticed that the roof lines above his eye level seemed to angle down and the lines below his eye level seemed to be angling up, converging on the horizon in front of him.

We do see things in perspective but when there is 40 feet of real space it is easier to accept the view than when this view is translated onto the space of twelve inches of flat paper.

The horizon is where the earth meets the sky, but without that reference in a classroom, the horizon is at the individual's eye level. Perspective drawing follows a certain number of rules. Once the students accept and follow these rules, creating space in a drawing becomes much easier. In perspective, lines vanish to a point on the horizon and objects get smaller the further they are away from us or the closer they are to the horizon.

The second rule in perspective drawing is that the students must not move their heads. The position of the head and the view of the eyes must remain stationary and in a fixed direction throughout the drawing. If they move their heads the perspective changes.

This first perspective drawing will be drawn in a classroom, where the horizon is located at eye level. All students will have a different horizon line, as the location depends on the height of their eyes. After explaining that the horizon line in the room is at eye level, walk around the room to emphasize where each student's horizon is located. Using a yardstick, stand across from a student, and holding the yardstick above her eye level, ask the student to keep her head in one place and focus her eyes straight in front of herself.

Start the yardstick above her eye level and slowly lower it, holding it horizontally until she stops you at her eye level. When she stops you, that is her horizon line. It is helpful to walk around the room asking the students to do this exercise with you so that each section of the room understands what you are talking about. It also helps the students to understand where the horizon line is located.

Perspective is hard for young students to grasp; before fifth grade go very slowly. Third graders should not be forced to follow the rules of perspective to a 'T' because this interferes with their natural creative abilities, which need to develop before they get into the technical side of art with all the rules of drawing. Start the third graders with the Overlapping Shapes exercise. Do the exercise, Perspective I, before you do this one.

Andrew Rowlett, Grade 4, One-point Perspective Landscape

USING THE HORIZON LINE AND THE VANISHING POINT

SUPPLIES

1. HB pencils
2. 12" x 18" white drawing paper
3. Shoe boxes or small boxes, one per student

At the top of the page—about one-third of the way down—have the students draw a horizontal line. This line represents the horizon line they can see in the room. The vanishing point is somewhere on the horizon line and its placement will be determined by the lines that will be drawn to it. There will be many vanishing points. Every object drawn will have its own vanishing point.

Lines below the horizon vanish up to the vanishing point and lines above the horizon vanish down to the vanishing point. In a one-point perspective all the lines forming the sides of an object vanish to one point. In a drawing of a house, the sides of the house that are square or straight on to the viewer are made of horizontal and vertical lines. Only the lines receding into space, which are diagonal lines, go to the VP (vanishing point).

To help the students understand perspective take a small box and pick a student to demonstrate with. Hold the box in front of the student so he or she can see the top, the front, and one side. Don't turn the box at a 45-degree angle to the student; turn the box only enough to see one side. The box is now below the horizon line, below eye level. Ask the student to hold up the left or right arm, depending on which side she or he sees the side of the box on. This is the same direction in which students will draw the side of the box on their papers. Continue around the room asking students in each section of the room the same question so all students can see what you are talking about.

Arrange the room so that each student has the above view of a box. Place the students 4 to 5 feet away. Place the box so they can see the top the front and one side. Ask them to draw the front of the box on their papers below the horizon line they drew. Start drawing the box from the front. To find the angle or the direction of the receding lines, have the students hold their pencils at arm's length in front of themselves lining the pencils up with the top edge of the box that is going away from them. The angle of the pencil is the angle of the line they need to draw receding from the front corner of the box all the way back to the horizon line. When the diagonal meets the horizon, that is where the vanishing point is, and all other lines on the box must angle over to that point. The receding lines do not need to end on the vanishing point; they need only taper in, heading eventually to a single point.

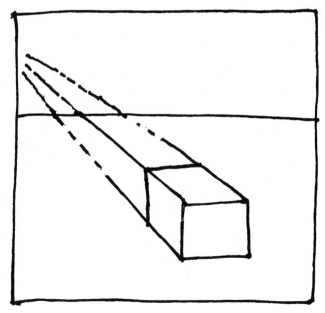

Diagram V: Horizon Line and Vanishing Point

Once all four lines are drawn, the students must decide where to cut the top of the box off. They must judge the amount of space to leave on the paper to represent the top of the box. Draw a horizontal line that is parallel to horizontal line to establish the back of the box between the two parallel lines, (Diagram V).

Cardboard boxes, hard-body suitcases, old steamer trunks or tissue boxes are good subjects to use for this exercise. Although artists prefer hand-drawn lines, the students should use rulers until they can angle their lines to a vanishing point.

SUMMARY OF STEPS

1. Discuss the horizon line.
2. Lines below the horizon vanish up.
3. Lines above the horizon vanish down.
4. Lines vanish to one point.
5. Draw a box in perspective.
6. Keep the head still.

GOALS

To understand perspective, and develop skills in translating three-dimensional subjects onto a two-dimensional piece of paper. This exercise improves critical thinking skills, and hand-eye coordination.

Grade 4, Glencoe School, One-point Perspective

Giorgio de Chirico, Italian, 1888–1978, *Piazza,* graphite on paper, 1914, 27.1 x 20 cm. Gift of Mary and Leigh Block, 1988.141.35. Photograph © 1995, The Art Institute of Chicago, 1988. All rights reserved.

BEGINNING LANDSCAPE:
A ONE-POINT PERSPECTIVE

BRIEF OVERVIEW

For this exercise you may want to put up a large piece of paper or piece of tag board. With a black felt pen, draw the steps for the students to follow. Once they understand the concept and process, they can introduce all kinds of variations to their drawings.

In perspective drawing, objects in the foreground are larger than objects in the background. Lines above the horizon vanish down and lines below the horizon vanish up. The top and bottom lines of one plane (as for a row of trees or poles) vanishes to one point on the horizon. One side of a house would be a plane.

Jonathan Rowlett, Grade 4, Charcoal and Wash

THE SETUP

Have the students draw a horizontal line across the center of their papers. Put a vanishing point on the horizon in the middle of the paper (indicate that point with a small mark). From the front edge of the paper, draw a diagonal line to the vanishing point. Move four inches to six inches away from this first line and draw another diagonal line from the paper's front edge to the vanishing point (see Diagram I).

From the top edge of the paper draw a line down to the vanishing point, which will be above the horizon. Draw a second line from the top of the paper to the vanishing point, above the horizon line (see Diagram II).

The students now have two cone shapes on their papers in which to start two rows of trees—one on each side. Start at the front of the paper. Draw a tree to fit in the widest area of the cone from top to bottom (see Diagram III). Moving back along the bottom diagonal select a spot a couple of inches away from the first tree and draw a second tree. Move back another inch and draw a third tree between the top and bottom lines.

Rule of Perspective:

The bases of the trees, from this point of view, are placed one behind another. Each base is placed up the page a little higher than the one in front of it. Do this same procedure between the second set of lines on the paper.

Drawing these vanishing lines gives the students top and bottom lines to fit the trees between, creating the appearance of trees receding in space.

Rule of Perspective :

Things appear smaller as they move away from us. Thus each tree is shorter and smaller as they move back to the horizon. The students can make as many rows of trees as will fit on the paper.

SUPPLIES

1. 6B, 3B, and HB drawing pencils
2. 12" x 18" white drawing paper
3. Rulers

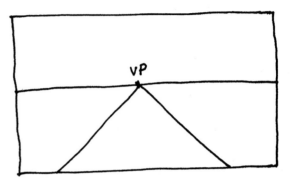

Diagram I

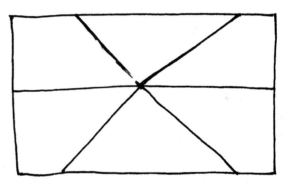

Diagram II

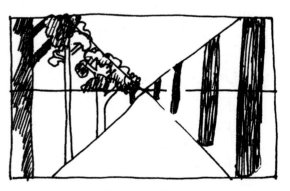

Diagram III

 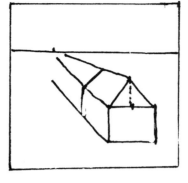 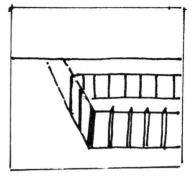

Diagram IV   Diagram V   Diagram VI

To draw clouds, start with small clouds at the horizon; each row that moves up and away from the horizon increases in size. The clouds at the top of the paper are the largest.

To draw a house, start by drawing a rectangular box in one-point perspective. To add the roof, find the center of the front wall and mark it, then make a mark above it the height the roof should be drawn. To shape the front of the roof, draw two diagonal lines from the top point one to each of the front corners on the box.

To form the roof top draw a diagonal line from the top point of the roof back to the same vanishing point used for the side of the box. Finish drawing the roof by adding two more lines, one from the roof top to the front corner of the box and one from the roof to the back corner of the box.

To draw a fence, draw two horizontal lines, one for the top of the fence, the other for the base line of the fence. To establish the top and bottom of the side of the fence, draw two diagonal lines receding to a vanishing point on the horizon, one from the top point and one from the bottom point of the first two horizontal lines. The lines do not need to meet at a point on the horizon, they need only to taper together so that at some point out in space they would meet. The fence posts are vertical lines both in the front and on the side. Use a ruler, to help keep the lines at 90 degrees to the bottom edge of the paper.

GOALS

To develop an understanding of the rules of perspective for translating the space in a landscape into the two-dimensional space of the paper. This exercise involves critical thinking skills and decision making. Doing this exercise increases awareness and perception.

SUMMARY OF STEPS

1. Draw a horizon line.
2. Place a VP on the horizon.
3. Draw two lines below vanishing to the horizon.
4. Draw two lines vanishing down to the horizon.
5. Draw all lines to one VP.
6. Start the trees at the front near the paper's edge.
7. Draw the trees between top and bottom lines.
8. Draw clouds in lines from the horizon up.
9. Draw a house.
10. Draw a fence.

Jeremy Bergmark, Grade 4, One-point Perspective Landscape

TWO-POINT PERSPECTIVE
Foundation Exercise

BRIEF OVERVIEW

More often than not you will need to use two-point perspective. One-point works well in a landscape, but a still life needs two-point perspective. If the students understand two-point perspective, setting up a still life is a lot easier because they can draw from various angles instead of being able to draw only objects placed directly in front of them.

Have the students look at the box before they start drawing. Ask the students to raise and point their arms at the angle of the right side, and then do the same for the left side. The angle of their arms is exactly the angle they should follow to draw the lines for the sides of the box.

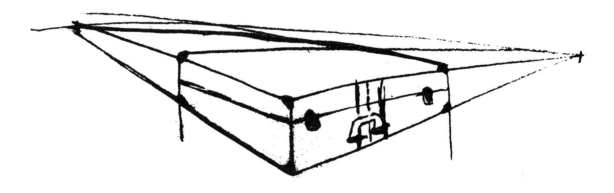

Amanda Chiavini, Grade 5, Two-point Perspective

SUPPLIES
1. 6B, 3B, and HB drawing pencils
2. 12" x 18" white drawing paper
3. Rulers

THE SETUP

Set cardboard boxes with lids closed at 45-degree angles on a table in front of the students. Use as many setups as necessary to keep the students within five to six feet of the setup.

In two-point perspective there are two vanishing points on the horizon. One side of the box vanishes to the left and one side vanishes to the right.

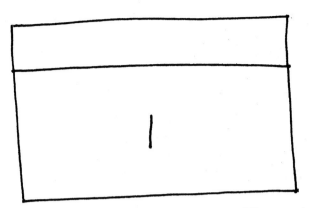

Diagram I

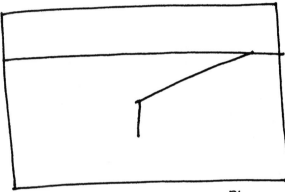

Diagram II

The boxes should be placed below the students' eye level to start.

Diagram I: Draw a horizon line one third of the way down from the top of the paper. Remember the horizon line is located at the student's eye level. Now draw a vertical line for the front corner of the box and locate it below the horizon. The line also represents the height of the box.

Diagram II: Draw a diagonal line from the top of the vertical line to the horizon at the angle at which the box is sitting. Remember the students can determine the angle by holding their pencils up in front of themselves and lining them up with the top and bottom edges of the box. The angle of the pencil is the angle to draw on the paper.

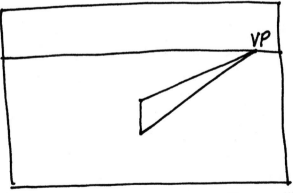

Diagram III

Diagram III: After drawing the top line, draw the bottom line for this first side.

Diagram IV: To draw the other side, draw a diagonal line to the horizon from the bottom and then the top of the vertical line. Both lines of each side must vanish to the same point. At first the students should draw to an exact point, but as they practice making other boxes they only need to angle the lines in the same direction; they do not need to make the lines meet at a point on the paper. The VP can be farther out in space. It can often make a box look warped to draw to a point that is too close.

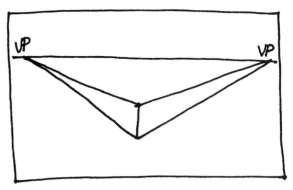

Diagram IV

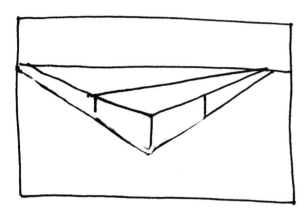

Diagram V

Diagram V: The students should now decide the length of both sides, by drawing a vertical line between the two receding top and bottom lines.

Diagrams V and VI: To draw the top surface of the box, draw a line from the back right corner to the left vanishing point. Next draw a line from the back left corner to the right vanishing point.

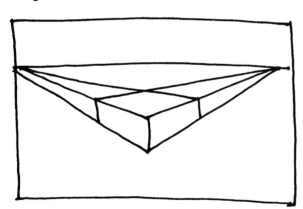

Diagram VI

GOALS

To practice and understand two-point perspective, developing critical thinking and decision making skills. To broaden the students technical skill in translating space. To improve measuring skills.

SUMMARY OF STEPS: BELOW THE HORIZON

1. Draw a horizon line one third of the way down.
2. Draw a vertical line under the horizon to start the box.
3. Draw two diagonal lines to a VP on the horizon on the right, one from top, and one from the bottom of the vertical line.
4. Repeat on the left side.
5. Draw the top with a diagonal line first from back right corner to left VP.
6. Now draw a diagonal line from back left corner to VP on right.

THE BOX AS SEEN ABOVE THE HORIZON

If you have boxes of the same size, stack them up to be one pillar whose top is above the horizon or eye level. Otherwise put something on the table to raise the boxes up or perhaps have the students sit on the floor and look up at the boxes. If the students are looking up at a table, the table top is the horizon line.

Lines above the horizon vanish down. It's best if the bottom of the box is placed below eye level and the top is above the horizon.

Diagram I: Place a horizon line in the middle of the paper. Draw the first vertical line across the horizon. The length of the line is the height of the box.

Diagram II: Find the angle of the bottom line on the right and draw a diagonal line to the horizon. Find the angle of the bottom of the box on the left and draw a diagonal line to the horizon on the left.

Diagram III: Look at the top of the box and figure the angle down to the horizon. Draw a line from the center line down to the horizon. Repeat for the other top line.

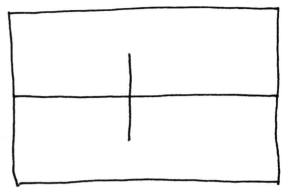

Diagram I

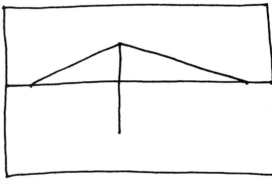

Diagram II

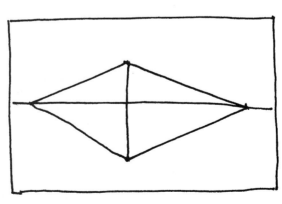

Diagram III

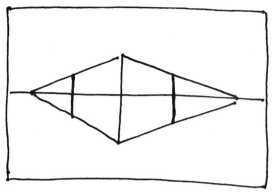

Diagram IV

Diagram IV: Use a vertical line to cut the back of the box off to the size needed to reflect the size of the box being drawn.

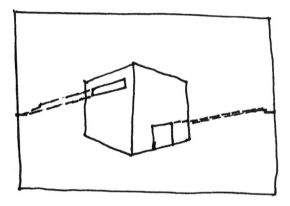

Diagram V

Diagram V: If this box were a building with windows, the lines for the top and bottom of the windows would also vanish to the same VP; all lines on the same side or same plane vanish to the same VP. Have the students draw two lines to the horizon for the windows and then use vertical lines to build windows in the side of the building. The doors are below the horizon and are constructed the same way, with lines vanishing up to the horizon.

MULTIPLE VANISHING POINTS

Notice in the drawing of the chair on the facing page that the chair is in two-point perspective and the boxes are also in two point perspective, but they all have different vanishing points. Take a piece of tracing paper and extend the lines to the horizon off the boxes and the chair. You may want to copy this drawing and let each student trace the receding lines to the horizon to help them understand perspective better.

SUMMARY OF STEPS ABOVE THE HORIZON

1. Draw a horizon line on the paper.
2. Draw a vertical line across horizon.
3. Find the angle of the bottom right side.
4. Draw a line from the vertical line to right VP.
5. Find angle of bottom left side.
6. Draw a line from vertical to VP left.
7. Find angle of top down to horizon.
8. Draw a line from vertical line down to the horizon to VP.
9. Repeat for other side of top.
10. Use vertical lines for back walls.

Drawing I, University Student Drawing, Multiple-point Perspective

HOUSES AND BUILDINGS: TWO-POINT PERSPECTIVE

SUPPLIES

1. HB, 3B, 6B pencils
2. Rulers
3. White paper
4. Plastic eraser
5. Ink, pen
6. Brush and wash

BRIEF OVERVIEW

The exercise in Two-point Perspective should be done before this one. Houses and buildings are drawn in two-point perspective. In two-point perspective there will be two points on the horizon to draw to. All the lines on the left of the building will vanish to a point on the left and all the lines to form the right side of the building will vanish to a point on the right.

It will be easiest to start out with the house drawn below the horizon. All the lines for the house will vanish up to the horizon. After the students draw this first house below the horizon, they can try one whose roof is above the horizon.

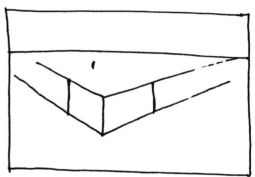

Below the Horizon: Diagram I

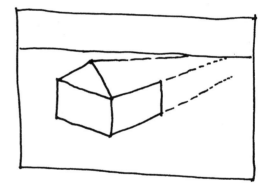

Below the Horizon: Diagram II

THE SETUP

Establish a horizon line. Draw a vertical line for the corner of the building the height the building will be before the roof goes on. Draw this line below the horizon. Next draw a base line to the horizon line on the left and then the right (see Diagram I).

Draw a top line to the horizon first to the left and then to the right. It looks like they are constructing a box. Determine the length of both sides with a vertical line between the vanishing diagonals for the back of the house (see Diagram I).

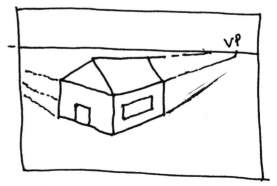

Below the Horizon: Diagram III

To add the roof find the center of the front side and mark it. Then make a mark above that center point the height of the roof. To form the front of the roof, draw a diagonal line from the height mark to the top right corner and one to the left top corner (see Diagram II).

To complete the roof, draw a line to the vanishing point from the center top point for the top of the roof. To draw the back edge of the roof use a line drawn at the same angle as the line is for the front edge.

Now decide where to place windows and draw a top and bottom line to the VP on the side where they are to be placed. Fit the vertical lines in to frame the shape of the windows. Decide where to place the door and draw a line to the VP for the top. The sides of the door are vertical lines. Remember, lines above the horizon vanish down and lines below the horizon vanish up.

HOUSES ABOVE THE HORIZON

Draw a horizon line and place a vertical line across it. This is the corner of the house. The base lines for the building will vanish up to the horizon and the roof lines will vanish down to it. To form the sides, draw two lines on each side to the VP, one from the top and one from the bottom of the vertical line. Find the center of the front side of the house and draw two diagonals from the height mark to

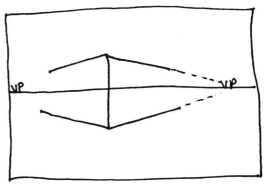

Above the Horizon: Diagram I

the corners of the roof. After the front triangle is on, draw a line from the crown point to the horizon. To make the roof look as if it sits over the house, extend the lines for the sides of the roof diagonal out a little bit.

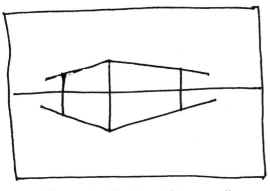

Above the Horizon: Diagram II

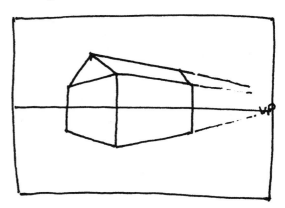

Above the Horizon: Diagram III

135

VALUE OPTIONS

The exercise warmup for ink drawing in Section Two should precede this one. To add value and texture, use pen, ink, brushes, and wash on the drawing. The pen and the black ink can be used to create texture for grass, dirt, leaves, bushes, tile walkways, bricks, shingles, and bark chips. Surfaces like the walls, the columns, and the sidewalks will improve with a few washes over them. The doors and windows look good in all black. The following page has a number of choices for roof lines, and columns, and window shapes that you can copy and hand out for the students to use to alter their houses.

Amanda Chiavini, Grade 5,
Two-point Perspective

GOALS

To increase the students' understanding of two-point perspective. To give the students a practical application of two-point perspective. To develop hand-eye coordination and visual skills in interpreting space.

SUMMARY OF STEPS

1. Draw a horizon line.
2. Draw a vertical line below the horizon.
3. Draw the left side with lines to left VP.
4. Draw the right side with lines to right VP.
5. Use a vertical line for the back of the house.
6. Mark the height of roof at the center of the front side of the house.
7. Draw two lines one to each front corner from the top center mark.
8. Draw a line to VP from the peak of the roof.
9. Cut end of roof line off with a diagonal line in back.
10. Add doors and windows.

MUCH OF OUR ARCHITECTURE COMES FROM THE GREEKS & ROMANS

3 CLASSIC GREEK ORDERS OF ARCHITECTURE

COLUMN OR POST

POST AND BEAM

COLONNADE

DORIC

IONIC

CORINTHIAN

KEYSTONE

ARCH

ARCADE

ROMAN   GOTHIC

TRUSS USED IN BRIDGES OR ROOFS

TRIANGLES WHEN PUT IN A CIRCLE CONE

ARCHES WHEN PUT IN A CIRCLE DOME

POSTS AND BEAMS BECOME A ROTUNDA

GABLE   HIP   MANSARD   GAMBREL   SHED
SOME TYPES OF ROOFS

DOUBLE-HUNG   CASEMENT   LEADED GLASS CASEMENT   DORMER   BAY WINDOW WITH PANELED DOOR
SOME TYPES OF WINDOWS

DETAILS:

BALUSTER

DENTILS

GREEK FRET

BRACKET

SCROLLS

EGG AND DART

137

Abraham Walkowitz, American, 1880–1965, *Six Figures*, ca. 1920, pencil and watercolor. Muscarelle Museum of Art, College of William and Mary in Virginia.

DARK TO LIGHT: PERSPECTIVE

BRIEF OVERVIEW

This exercise uses ink. Ink drawing relies on a layering process. The white of the paper is the lightest value in the drawing. Every wash that is added darkens the area it is put on. This is called working from light to dark. The procedure for mixing ink washes is covered in the exercise Warm-up for Ink Drawing in Section Two.

The students may make up a scene, or you may want to show them pictures by artists or photographers out of magazines or out of their text-books on history and geography. Have them select a landscape.

Begin the drawing with the HB pencil and using light pressure. The students draw a very light outline around the areas in the drawing that in the end they want left white. This maps out areas to save. In landscape drawing the students work from the back to the front of the drawing. The students will use the first light wash on the clouds and hills at the horizon.

In the end the foreground should be dark and the background much lighter, giving the impression that the mountains and clouds on the horizon are far away and faint in the distance.

This exercise is designed for students to practice building ink washes, and to create a sense of space through value change from front to back. The exercise in the Perspective section of the book on One-point Perspective: Landscape can help the students to compose their landscapes but it's not important that they have the landscape in perspective.

THE SETUP

Using the HB pencil, draw a border one inch around the edge of the paper. Each student then lightly maps out in pencil the composition of the landscape (Diagram I). Use two or three large trees in the foreground to frame the space. Place the top of the tree at the top of the page and the bottom of the tree at the bottom of the piece of tag board. The next element could be a house or barn seen through the trees. Draw the base line for the house two to three inches from the bottom of the paper. The top of the building should be five to six inches from the top of the paper. Add the mountains and foothills behind the house at about two to three inches from the top of the paper .

It's not that important in this exercise that the perspective is correct; in this exercise we focus on using ink to create space, working from dark in the foreground to light in the background.

The wax is used for texture and as a resist in the drawing. Take the wax and rub it *firmly* over the grass area in front of the house, at the top of the trees in the leaf areas, and anywhere else the students would like a rough, irregular texture.

Outline in pencil areas to be left white. Mix the first light gray wash with a little ink and water. Compressed charcoal may be used to outline the drawing and to reinforce linear areas, like fences and house outlines before and after adding the wash. Compressed charcoal works well on top of wash for grass lines. Compressed charcoal will thin with water and can be added on top of dry washed areas.

Place the first wash on the entire drawing, leaving only the white areas. Let the wash dry before adding a second wash. The students should be working with small amounts of wash in their brushes and using only the end or tip of the brush. Keep the brush wet to avoid a bushy, unuseable brush. The brush looks like an electrified cartoon cat when it dries out!

SUPPLIES
1. 12" x 18" tag board
2. HB pencil
3. Quill brush
4. Compressed charcoal
5. Wax
6. 4 small jars or dishes
7. Water
8. India ink bottles or small dishes
9. Paper towels for drips and wiping off brushes

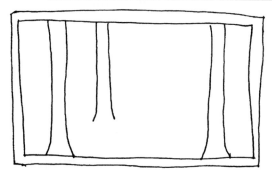

Diagram I

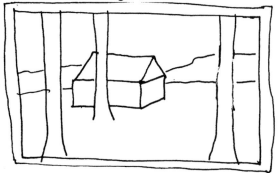

Diagram II

Diagram III

While they wait for the wash to dry, mix a second wash by adding a little more ink to the first wash mixture. Use the second wash for shading on the foothills and clouds. Put some on the grass and light side of the trees and light side of the house. Save the second wash.

For a third and darker wash empty half of the second wash into a new jar or dish, and add more ink with the tip of the brush to this new jar. The students now have a gray (the second wash) and a darker gray (the third wash) to use.

Using the third wash, cover the tops and trunks of the trees, parts of the ground in front of the house (that has wax on it) and the roof of the house. Darken this third wash again, making wash number four, with another drop of ink and cover the areas to be dark in the foreground, the trees, one side of the house, and the shadows.

Using the black ink at full strength with no water, darken three-fourths of the tree trunks, the underside of the top of the tree, put some shadows on the ground in front of and beside the house, and select other areas to be dark.

You may use as many wash solutions as you like. Four washes and the black keeps the exercise simple so you all can get used to the ink. The students can add black brush strokes to the roof to texture it or black strokes to the ground. As long as the ink is mixed with water it is going to dry lighter than the full strength ink. Any wash on top of another will look darker because they are building up.

Sarah Dobbins, Grade 4, Dark to Light Perspective

GOALS

The students must plan their drawing from back to front, which challenges their previous sense of space. They must make decisions and think critically. They develop technical skill by watching the ink interact and build. In the end they can see how perspective is achieved through value change across the surface of the paper.

SUMMARY OF STEPS

1. Draw a border on the paper.
2. Draw a landscape.
3. Mix the first wash.
4. Map out light areas.
5. Rub wax firmly over texture areas.
6. Place the first wash on back and foreground.
7. Let it dry; mix the second wash.
8. Leave background.
9. Put the second wash on middle area.
10. Save second wash.
11. Put the third wash on trees, grass, one side of house.
12. Use the second and third washes over each other.
13. Add the black ink to front trees and shadows.

Kathe Köllwitz, German, 1867–1945, *Sorrowful Woman,* charcoal on buff-colored paper faded from blue. The Frederick and Lucy S. Herman Foundation. Muscarelle Museum of Art, College of William and Mary in Virginia.

Amanda Chiavini, Grade 4, Still Life with Foreshortened Handles

FORESHORTENING
Foundation Exercise

BRIEF OVERVIEW

Perspective is the process used to represent the change in size of objects as they recede in space. Foreshortening is a technique designed to represent an object that has been extended forward in space. The parts on the object must be contracted and layered to depict the object. In foreshortening, spatial relationships are compressed rather than extended. There is no flowing of one form into the other; each section must overlap the one behind it, and the distance between areas is reduced to inches for spaces that could be two feet long. Foreshortening produces an illusion of the object projecting forward. Any form seen head-on must be drawn foreshortened to create a realistic rendering.

Foreshortening may exaggerate the feeling of rapid movement into space and a spatial projection of objects or forms. Foreshortening is one of the hardest techniques in perspective to learn. It has no natural reference; nowhere in our education do we encounter or see foreshortening.

Foreshortening was developed in the Renaissance by artists to deal with the problems of drawing the human form when the view was down the form from the feet to the head, or down an arm projecting forward in space toward the artist.

Foreshortening is an extension of the process described in the lesson, Overlapping Shapes, only now it is overlapping parts of one shape—not one shape overlapping another.

THE SETUP

Because foreshortening is used mostly on the figure, it is difficult to find things to draw that are as dramatic. You have already experienced a foreshortening problem in the previous still life drawings with the handles and spouts on the pitchers. When a handle or spout is placed directly in front of the students, it is a very hard view to draw.

To start this exercise give each student one pitcher, a teakettle, or another object with projecting parts like handles to draw. Place the handle directly in front of the student's view. Draw the projecting part on the paper, starting with the shape in the front. Have them look at the form for a few minutes, studying exactly where the front part intersects the body of the kettle. Using diagonal lines connect the handle to the kettle by angling them up a little bit.

A reminder on using erasers: Ask the students to start with the HB pencil, drawing very lightly. Only after they attempt to draw the form and change the lines over and over should you offer them an eraser. Once they have the form as they think it should be, use the 3B to reinforce the light or top lines and the 6B to darken the under or bottom areas; 3B lines should be thin, and 6B lines should be thicker. Alternating lines from light to dark creates a sense of volume and weight in the drawing.

It is very important to maintain one view of the object. Everything changes if the students move their heads. Plan the drawing moving from the handle to the body of the pitcher. They must draw from the front shape to the back shape, adding each part on.

The Degas drawing on the facing page is a good example of foreshortening. The dancer's head is in front of her chest; notice how there is no space between the two. Foreshortening a subject means drawing what you really see—not what you know. We know the neck is four to six inches long, but in the drawing we can't see it so we can't draw it. Observation skills must be keen and precise in foreshortening, as the artist must look at exactly where each part intersects the section behind it. The proportions of each form are important. Have the students note how much bigger or smaller each succeeding section is compared with the one in front of it and the one behind it.

SUPPLIES

1. 12" x 18" white paper
2. HB, 3B, and 6B pencils
3. Plastic erasers
4. Photos (option)
5. Tracing paper (option)

Edgar Degas, French, 1834–1917, *Dancer Bending Forward,* charcoal with stumping heightened with white and yellow pastel with stumping, on blue laid paper, 1874-79, 46.2 x 30.4 cm. Mr. and Mrs. Martin A. Ryerson Collection, 1933.1230. Photograph © 1995. The Art Institute of Chicago. All rights reserved.

DRAWING OPTION I

Another way to help students understand foreshortening is to trace drawings like the Degas drawing. Collect some photos from magazines or make your own examples by taking photos of your students with their hands out in front of their faces or in front of their bodies. A student sitting in a chair leaning back with feet up on a stool is a good foreshortened view to use. Then let the students trace the photos on typing paper or tracing paper so they can experience how one shape overlaps the next.

DRAWING OPTION II

Good objects to use are cowboy boots, (looking from the bottom or sole up the boot), a bouquet of flowers, (looking at the stems first), wine bottles, (painted black or a color without their labels) lying down.

Lay the objects flat on the table, position the students so each one of them is looking down on the objects. To render an object lying down on a table, start the drawing near the bottom of the paper, and slowly and gradually draw the shape moving up the paper a little at a time. Each part or section is added on from front to back as you move up the paper. Often a dividing line must be drawn to separate one part from the section in front of it. This line is used to end the first form. It has nothing to do with outline or texture. The chin line on the Dancer by Degas is such a line as are the outlines on the arms.

GOALS

To develop the students' abilities to visually translate a foreshortened form. To improve and alter levels of perception. To increase the students' understanding of difficult perspectives. To improve critical thinking skills and visual awareness.

SUMMARY OF STEPS

1. Discuss foreshortening and overlapping forms.
2. Explain compressing forms.
3. Practice with one pitcher and the handle.
4. View the form from the handle or the spout.
5. Discuss Degas's drawing.
6. Do Option I.
7. Trace a foreshortened photo.
8. Do Option II.
9. Lay a form down.
10. Position students to look down the form.

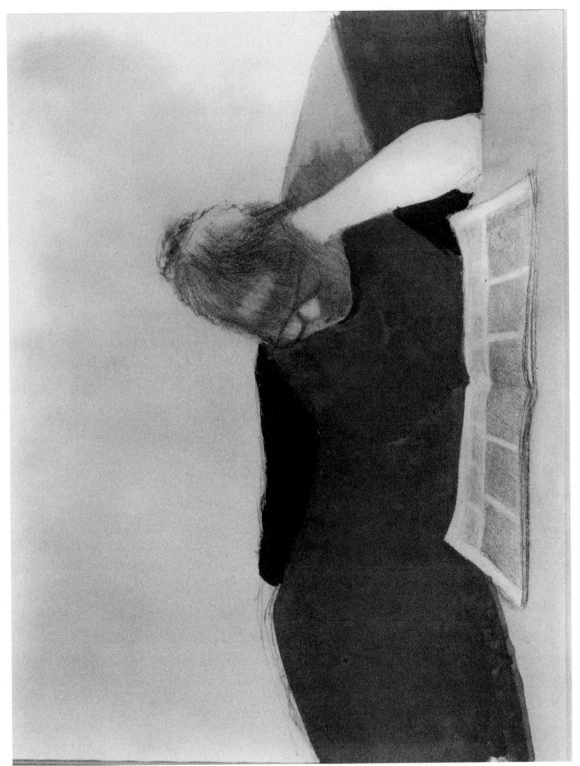

Robert Bechtle, *Nancy Reading*, 1965, graphite and watercolor on paper, 18 3/8" x 22 7/8" (46.7 x 58.1 cm). San Francisco Museum of Modern Art. Gift of Bill Bass, 75.184.

Cecil Hill, My Favorite Uncle, Texas 1947. Grid Enlargement

GRID TRANSFERS

BRIEF OVERVIEW

If you have a complicated scene or if you want to take something very small and enlarge it, you use a grid to transfer the images. Working with a grid allows you to transfer an image in exact proportions from a small image to a large image.

THE SETUP

Select a drawing, photo, or other image. The image should be at least two inches on a side. Divide the photo in half on both sides by finding the center point of each side and drawing a line between the two marks. Having two points to draw between will give you straight lines.

If the image to be copied is two inches on a side, divide it in half on both sides, making one-inch squares. Divide the one-inch squares in half. The photo is now halved and quartered.

To transfer the image at the same size, take a piece of paper that is also two inches on each side and halve and quarter it with light pencil lines. The original photo and the paper to transfer it to must be the same size and have the same divisions.

To increase the size of the image, multiply each side by the factor you wish to increase the drawing—two times, four times, six times. Thus a two-inch image enlarged four times would be transferred to a piece of paper eight inches on a side.

After the white paper has been divided in half and in fourths exactly as the original image has been divided, the students start transfering the lines and forms from each section to the matching sections on the paper. For example, if a piece of an object starts on the top and curves through the top quarter to the second quarter, copy and place that shape on the white paper in the same quarters.

SUPPLIES

1. HB, 3B, 6B pencils
2. Photo
3. Ruler
4. White paper

The grid transfer technique can be used to create a mural from small student drawings. You can draw a sketch of what you want painted on the wall, grid it off into halves and quarters and then grid off the wall or large paper with the same number of separations. Transfer the drawing section by section.

Be sure the paper and the wall have the same relative proportions. If the wall is 10 feet x 16 feet, when divided by two, it's 5 feet x 8 feet; when reduced again, it's 2 1/2 feet x 4 feet, or 30 inches x 48 inches, which can be reduced again to 15 inches x 24 inches. This is the size the piece of paper must be to proportionately transfer the images on to the wall from the drawing. Be sure you have the same number of divisions on both the wall and the paper. The larger the drawing, the more divisions you will need to make to help in the transfer.

GOALS

To improve students' hand-eye coordination and increase their understanding of space. This exercise depends on concentration and patience. It also involves knowledge of simple math.

SUMMARY OF STEPS

1. Select a photo or drawing.
2. Cut the paper to the same dimensions as the photo.
3. To increase a photo, increase the paper size proportionately.
4. Divide the photo in half, and then in fourths.
5. Divide the paper in half and fourths.
6. Transfer lines from one section of the photo at a time.
7. Transfer the shapes to the corresponding area on the paper.

SIGHT MEASURING:
USING A VIEWFINDER

BRIEF OVERVIEW

Translating real or three-dimensional space into a drawing or onto a two-dimensional surface is one of the hardest things to teach. Sight measuring, using a viewfinder, offers the students a physical relationship to understanding perspective.

Perspective assumes a fixed point of view, making it very important that the student's head and eyes remain stationary to keep the drawing in perspective. In addition to the viewing position, two other relationships are crucial:

1. The distance from the subject being drawn; objects appear larger or smaller in relation to their distance from the viewer.

2. The student's angle in relationship to the subject; the angle will change the perspective. If the students are directly in front or at the middle, they have a completely different perspective from that of a student sitting at an angle to the subject.

Perspective hinges on accepting that parallel lines moving away from us appear to converge at one point on the horizon. The point they meet at what is called the vanishing point. Other devices used to create a sense of perspective are overlapping forms, the reduction of the size of objects as they recede, and blurring of details seen in the distance.

This exercise will help the students understand what the picture plane is and how it operates in drawing. The picture plane can be thought of as an imaginary pane of glass directly in front of and between the artist and the subject matter. This imaginary glass is perpendicular to the artist's sight line in the same way as the drawing paper. Therefore, the paper and the picture plane are the same. To demonstrate how the picture plane frames the subject to be drawn, place a piece of plexiglas between a student and the subject and have the student draw what he or she can see through the glass. The plexiglas in this exercise is the picture plane; tracing the subject or scene may help the students to understand how we translate space in perspective to paper. An additional help might be a tilted drawing board placed in front of the students. Drawing from this angle can correct some of this visual dilemma, as it allows the students to continually look forward instead of looking down on their paper on a flat desk.

THE SETUP

A piece of plexiglas 12 inches or 18 inches square and a china marker are preliminary aids in perspective drawing. If the expense of plexiglas is too great, the students can draw directly on a window. The china marker will wash off with glass cleaner. The students must hold their heads and eyes in one position. Set the glass, at a fixed distance from the student's eyes, in front of a still life or some part of the room. They can close one eye and trace the scene enclosed by the glass. They should establish the location of the horizon line and if they are drawing a box or house, lightly extend the diagonals to the vanishing points.

If the glass is too close to the eye, objects in the foreground will be huge. Experiment with placing the plexiglas at different distances from the subject to see how their view of space changes. Ask the students to draw from an arm's length back.

SUPPLIES

1. HB, 3B pencils
2. 12" or 18" square white paper
3. A piece of plexiglas
4. Black china marker
5. 24" square piece of cardboard
6. String
7. Tape
8. Mat knife
9. Drawing board (optional)
10. Plastic eraser
11. Ruler

Place the glass on a piece of white paper to see the drawing. This device will help clarify perspective for the students. They can experience making converging lines and locating the vanishing point on the horizon. Have them make a drawing freehand of the same view.

SUMMARY OF STEPS

1. Discuss the devices of perspective.
2. Locate the subject through the plexiglas.
3. Draw the subject on glass with marker.
4. Locate the horizon and VP on glass.
5. Place the glass on paper to view.

MAKING A VIEWFINDER

A viewfinder is a piece of cardboard with a small square cut out of the center. Use a piece of cardboard approximately 24 inches or 30 inches square. The cut out opening should be approximately one inch square. Use two pieces of thin string to divide the opening in half vertically and horizontally. The students may use rulers to find the center of each side.

The string lines divide the scene or subject to be drawn. This procedure will help the students proportion the drawing. The students should draw on a square piece of paper. Using an HB pencil have the students divide their papers in half on both sides—creating four equal areas or quadrants. The lines on the paper relate directly to the string lines on the viewfinder.

The students now hold the viewfinder out in front of themselves, closing one eye and searching around the room or out the window, framing scenes until they find one they want to draw. They should experiment with the distance the viewfinder is placed from the eyes: try the viewfinder close and then far away.

Once they locate what they want to draw, fix the viewfinder in place. Tape it to a chair or tape it to the window. If they have a drawing board they can tape it to the top of the drawing board.

Transfer one quadrant at a time. Have the students look at what is in the top left quadrant and draw those forms in the top left quadrant of their papers. Do the same for the lines and forms in the other three quadrants. If something intersects the string halfway down, then it will intersect the line on the paper halfway down. Transfer the information by referring to the location in the viewfinder and then placing the information in the same place on the paper. The drawing will be larger than the area of the viewfinder's opening, thus the students must judge how long a shape is proportionately to the space it occupies in the one inch opening.

GOALS

To develop a better understanding of perspective. To increase the students' abilities in translating and transferring three-dimensional space into two-dimensional space. To improve perception and observation skills—developing new ways of seeing.

SUMMARY OF STEPS FOR VIEWFINDER

1. Make a viewfinder.
2. Divide the viewfinder in four equal sections.
3. Divide paper in quadrants.
4. Pick a subject.
5. Fix viewfinder.
6. Transfer the subject quadrant by quadrant.

Neil Jansen, Grade 5, Drawing Standing Up. (Finished Drawing on p. 117.)

Constantin Brancusi, French, born Rumania, 1876–1957, *The Studio*, Black ink on tan wove paper laid down on cream wove card, c. 1918, 43 x 35.4 cm. Bequest of Mrs. Gilbert W. Chapman, 1981.149. Photograph © 1995. The Art Institute of Chicago. All rights reserved.

YOUR NAME IN LIGHTS

BRIEF OVERVIEW

This exercise is another way to approach one-point perspective. The vanishing point may be placed above the letters or under them or off to one side. The students may leave the lines drawn all the way to the vanishing point, like the Ed Ruscha example, or they may draw lines at a selected distance that echo the front lines. This latter choice creates large, deep block letters.

THE SETUP

To start, students write their names in large gothic block letters on a piece of paper. If they make the letters too small the vanishing lines will get all tangled up, and it makes separating the planes more difficult later. Leave at least a half inch between each letter. If the letters are placed too close together, it is harder to draw the vanishing lines.

The round letters like the *D, O, P,* and *S* are the hardest to square off. The students should use a diagonal line to form the curve. Letters like *O, A, P,* and *Q* also have an interior shape that the students will need to draw. The interior shape echoes the exterior edge.

Before they start they should consider where to place the letters on the paper. After they have the letters laid out, they select the location for the vanishing point. Have them place a mark on the paper for the vanishing point.

SUPPLIES

1. 12" x 18" or 18" x 24" white paper
2. Ruler
3. Plastic eraser
4. Pencil sharpener
5. Ink or felt-tip pens
6. Colored felt-tip pens

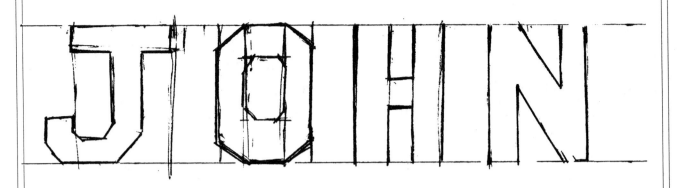

To form the letters, draw two lines 1 inch to 2 inches apart for the top and bottom of the letters. Measure off equal units of 1 inch to 1 1/2 inches along the bottom line. Leave 1/2 inch between each unit. Then construct the letter inside the measured space. Start with the vertical sides of each letter first, and then shape the interior of the letter. Letters needing interiors are O, B, A, and so on.

Using a ruler, draw lines from each corner point on the letter to the vanishing point. If the line runs into the letter next to it, stop the line. Don't let a vanishing line cross a letter. The vanishing lines may go from all corners on the letter whether the corner is inside or outside.

When all the vanishing lines are drawn, the students will have created planes for each side or surface on the letters. They should separate these planes with a value change; they can rotate between black and white, or they can use color and change the color on each plane. Adding value or color will accentuate the sense of the planes receding and add more weight to the drawing.

ANOTHER OPTION

The students can cut the letters off to make large block letters. The letters will seem to be standing up like sculptures. They may choose any length for this sculptural form.

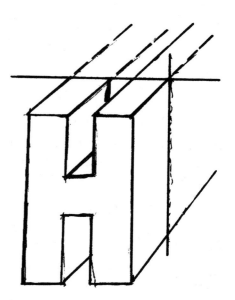

They can also shade in alternating planes or draw a landscape behind and around the letters—putting them in a setting.

GOALS

This is a simple exercise to increase the students' understanding of one-point perspective. It is a clear example of surfaces as planes. It improves their hand-eye coordination as well as their technical skill.

SUMMARY OF STEPS

1. Write a word in block letters.

2. Make large letters.

3. Pick a vanishing point.

4. Draw lines from each corner of a letter to the vanishing point.

5. Select a value for each plane.

6. Students may choose to shape letters with a back line.

Edward Ruscha, *Trademark 2*, 1962, ink, pencil, and oil on paper, 8 3/4" x 14 1/4" (24.8 x 36.2 cm.). San Francisco Museum of Modern Art. Purchased through a gift of Dr. And Mrs. Robert Dean, 81.99, San Francisco.

Georges Braque, *Vase, Palette and Mandolin*, 1936, oil. 32" x 32". San Francisco Museum of Modern Art. Gift of W.W. Crocker, 44.2641.

FLATTENED PERSPECTIVE

BRIEF OVERVIEW

This exercise is based on Cubism, a style of art pioneered by Pablo Picasso and Georges Braque in the first decade of the twentieth century—noted for the geometry of its forms, its fragmentation of the object, and its increasing abstraction, including the deliberate absence of Renaissance perspective.

Georges Braque's, *Vase, Palette and Mandolin*, painted in 1936, is a strong example of the flattened perspective Cubism developed. The objects in the composition seem to have been flattened as if they were run over by a steamroller. The planes are not only flattened, they are often pulled apart and displaced so half of a plane may be placed on the right side and the other half is attached to the left side. Areas are cut in parts and shifted to fit unevenly back together. The outside edge of the work is mis-shapen and irregular.

In the cylinder study we learned how to create an ellipse to create the illusion of the top of a vase or a bottle; now the Cubists return to the full circle—tilting an open top at the viewer that doesn't fit with the rest of the vase or bottle. They were interested in the object from all sides. They would analyze the objects of their compositions in terms of flattening them to the picture plane. Nothing would be perceived as moving back in space and more often than not the compositions seem to come forward into the viewer's space. From 1907 on, painting would no longer be about representation; it would now primarily be about painting as itself. Modernism was born.

One way to demonstrate the Cubist approach to making a painting is to take a cardboard box and open it up, flattening all the sides flush to the table. To define the individual sides of the box, paint on them or use texture marks before you flatten it, the students can then see the sides in the flattened form. It would be like taking the top and the bottom ends off a soup can and setting them down next to the flattened soup can. All the images and objects are on the same plane and flat on the picture plane.

Some of the objects used in the cubist collages and paintings were made up. Braque once said that he and Picasso particularly liked to use the guitar and the mandolin in their compositions, but that neither one had ever had either instrument in his studio.

THE SETUP

Loosely set up a still life of bottles, cans, books, candlesticks, glasses, or vases with newspaper headlines sitting beside them or under them. Bring out a violin or a guitar and set in on a table. Assemble various materials to collage—magazines, newspapers, contact papers of wood or marble surfaces, colored papers, and art supplies like ink and charcoal.

Ask the students to start by making a drawing that relates to the still life on paper or tag board. Then have them cut it up and reassemble it on a cardboard support. They may assemble and glue down materials with their drawings. They may add texture, either real or simulated. Braque often added sand to his paint to rough it up.

Some Cubist collages were assembled in a spiral fashion—with one piece added and overlapped to the next in a circular manner. Other compositions were stacked in a gridlike formation, and some were fitted into an oval shape instead of the traditional rectangle.

If students are going to add heavy things, they should work on cardboard or cardboard covered with white paper that has been glued to it. Tag board will take some working but not a lot. The tag board may also be glued to the cardboard for support.

They may draw any object or form that is in the room or that they have in their memories. They may add real materials or make up a texture. All objects must be drawn as flattened, the table or ground should be separated and shifted to eliminate any sense of depth of receding space. Putting a black outline around shapes also flattens them.

SUPPLIES

1. Tag board
2. Cardboard
3. Pencils, ink and charcoal
4. Pen and Brush
5. Collage materials
6. Glue

GOALS

The students must concentrate on eliminating depth and perspective. Their technical skills are improved with the cutting, pasting, and drawing. They must plan and select materials for their compositions developing decision-making skills. Their understanding of space and plane should be enhanced.

SUMMARY OF STEPS

1. Discuss the qualities of Cubism.

2. Set up a loose still life with objects placed around the room.

3. Draw objects as if they were flat.

4. Add things from memory.

5. Cut drawing up and reassemble. Shift the outlines of the objects.

6. Add other materials to the drawing.

7. Glue the collage to cardboard.

Caleb Ruecker, Grade 4, Ink Line Drawing

Francis Picabia, French 1879–1953, *Entrance to New York,* watercolor over pencil, 1913, 75.6 x 55.5 cm., Alfred Stieglitz Collection, 1949.576. Photograph © 1995. The Art Institute of Chicago. All rights reserved.

SECTION FOUR:
Space/Shape/Plane

Francisco José de Goya y Lucientes, *Regozyo (Mirth)*, gray and black wash on paper, 18" x 28 1/2".
Courtesy of the Hispanic Society of America, A3308. New York, New York.

COMPOSING SPACE: THE SPATIAL CHARACTERISTICS OF VALUE

BRIEF OVERVIEW

Of all the art elements, value is the strongest in manipulating two-dimensional space to create the illusion of three-dimensional space. Value may define light, structure, weight, or space in a drawing. To describe space, artists may follow nature in depicting light as it falls, or they can create a sense of space by manipulating light and dark.

The Francisco José de Goya y Lucientes drawing on the facing page called *Regozyo (Mirth)* is a gray and black wash on paper. It is a wonderful example of how value changes move the eye through space. Goya was the master of manipulating value to set the tone and create the feeling of space in his drawings. Goya starts the viewer with the sole of the shoe on the woman in the front; it's dark, then the foot is light, and the leg under her dress is gray. Then he leaves a white edge on the skirt with a dark value on her skirt up to the waist. The blouse is scumbled with deep shadows and the shawl in the middle is white. Her hair is black. The second person has a gray outfit on with a black kerchief and a white face. The value changes on the figure in the back have nothing to do with light and everything to do with creating a sense of space. He moves the viewer's eye in and out across the figure by changing from dark to white, then gray, then back to white, then to black, and so on.

By going from light to dark, dark to light, dark to gray he forces the eye to separate the forms and see them as separate spaces. Notice that there's no ground in the drawing. The figures float in the space; seeming to jump or dance.

THE SETUP

Arrange a collection of objects on a table. Bowls, cups, wine bottles (without labels), coke bottles, teapots, coffee pots, cans or vases of different heights and widths are possible choices. Place the objects in overlapping positions from the front to the back of the table. Have the students sit in a circle around the table. You may need two or three setups, depending on your class size.

In this drawing the students must decide if a form is black or white. The form may be entirely one value or half black and half white. If it is black, the space right next to it must be white, so if the space under the table is black, then the table top in the front is white. All spaces count—the objects, their shadows, the table top, the

SUPPLIES
1. 12" x 18" white paper
2. Compressed charcoal
3. HB pencil
4. Kneaded erasers
5. Plastic erasers
6. Tissues

Drawing I, Space in Terms of Light and Dark. College Student

space between the objects, and the space the students can see behind and in between the objects. They are to move across the drawing from the bottom of the paper to the top, filling it entirely. Each step of the way from the front to the back of the still life, they must make decisions on where to place the black and where to leave the white.

To start, have the students draw a line a few inches from the bottom edge of the paper. This line may be straight or curved, depending on the shape of the table. Draw the line across the entire sheet of paper to represent the front edge and the space just under the front edge of the table.

They may outline the objects in pencil before they start drawing with the charcoal. The pre-line drawing will give them a map of their choices. Use the compressed charcoal with light pressure to go over the objects that are to be black. With a tissue or a bare finger, rub the charcoal into the paper for a deeper, richer black—or use firm pressure. A second layer of charcoal can be added after a layer is rubbed.

Compressed charcoal does not erase very easily, but if there are too many smudges at the end of the drawing use the kneaded eraser to clean up the marks. The plastic eraser will remove some charcoal also. Don't give the students erasers until the page if filled. Ask them to consider each value choice carefully.

They are to make their decisions in terms of the space and placement of the objects. This has nothing to do with how light falls; that's another problem covered elsewhere. In a way it's a puzzle; each move and choice they make affects the next one.

SUMMARY OF STEPS

1. Arrange students around a still life.
2. Start the drawing under the edge of the table.
3. Outline six shapes from bottom to top.
4. Include foreground and background.
5. Choose black or white for each shape and space.
6. A shape may be half black and half white.
7. A white area must be next to a black area.
8. Erase smudges at the end to clean up drawing.

GOALS

To develop a better understanding of how the eye is directed across two-dimensional space by value change. To improve decision-making skills and critical thinking.

Drawing I, College Student, Balancing Space

DRAWING NEGATIVE SPACE

BRIEF OVERVIEW

Negative space may also be referred to as *empty space* or *interspace*. It is the space in between two positive spaces or the space around the objects in a still life. It is the space between the mountains in a landscape or the space between the tree branches you can look through. It is important space, because without it all positive space would cease to exist. Positive space without negative space is one big endless, shapeless blob. Seeing negative space, however, is difficult.

The distinction between positive and negative shapes on the picture plane—the two-dimensional surface on which the artist works—is that positive shapes are the objects drawn and negative shapes are the areas around and between the positive shapes. To draw negative shapes is to draw air. With a stepladder, for example, you can draw the sides and the rungs or steps on the ladder in outline or you can draw the space inside the rungs and leave the wooden or aluminum part as the white of the paper with no defining lines. The drawing in this lesson was constructed in exactly that manner. The artist drew one empty space after another—leaving the outline of the shapes out, but forming the shapes by drawing the space on either side.

SUPPLIES

1. 12" x 18" tag board
2. Vine charcoal
3. Chamois
4. Sumi ink
5. Brush
6. Kneaded eraser
7. Cup of water

THE SETUP

Select a misshapen or curvy object—a bicycle seat, rolled-edge vase, tennis shoe, boot, iron, bucket with the handle up—and place it on top of a box or stool or another object on a table. It is best to stack two shapely objects one on top of the other. Using the vine charcoal, the students draw only the silhouette by following the outline of the two objects. Place them in the middle of the paper. They fill the paper from the top to the bottom, running off the top and the bottom with the silhouette of the forms. Students should draw only around the outside edge without making any lines to define the insides of the shapes.

Have the students use the sumi ink and a damp brush to fill in all the negative space around the objects, leaving the shape of the objects the white of the paper. It's O.K. if some of the charcoal gets smudged on the white; it merely enhances or activates the positive area.

The students should not erase any lines until they have completed drawing the entire form. When the outline is finished any line left in the middle of the positive area may be removed with the chamois and kneaded eraser before adding the ink background.

Rinse the brush out in clear water.

GOALS

To develop the students' understanding of negative and positive space. To improve perception skills and develop a larger awareness of space. To improve visualizing skills.

SUMMARY OF STEPS

1. Explain positive and negative space.
2. Stack two objects together.
3. Students draw the silhouettes of the stacked forms.
4. Fill the page from top to bottom.
5. Run the shapes off the top and bottom.
6. Erase unwanted lines in positive space.
7. Ink in all negative space.

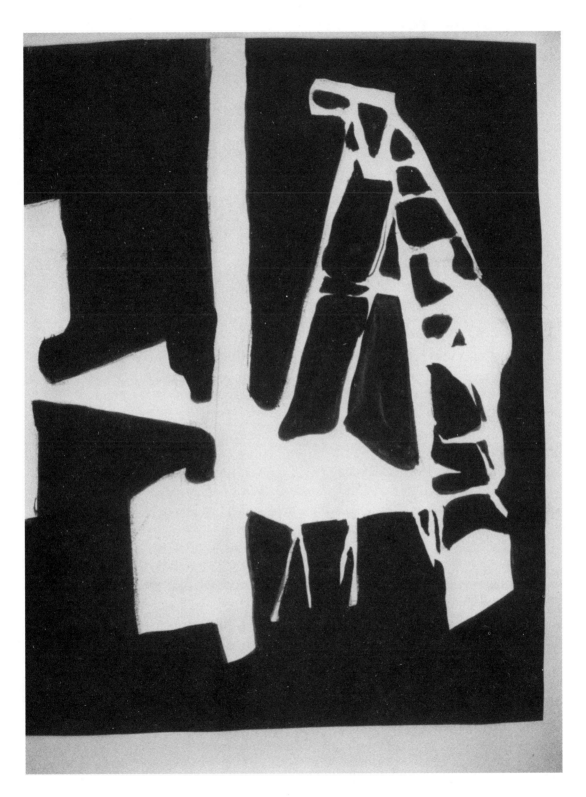

Drawing I, College Student, Ink, Model on a Ladder, Negative Space

DRAWING NEGATIVE SPACE II

BRIEF OVERVIEW

The subject to be drawn in this exercise is complicated. The students will need to take their time and study the setup a little before they start. It's like playing a visual add-on game; drawing empty space.

THE SETUP

In the middle of the room stack up chairs, tables, stools, or stepladders on top of each other, using poles or sticks to bridge across the open areas between chairs. It is important to keep space between the chairs and stools. Try not to let the stack get compacted. While arranging the stack try to keep it balanced between the open space and the objects.

The students can sit on the floor or, if there's room, arrange their desks around the mountain of chairs and stools in the center of the room. Have them keep their drawing arm free, leaning only on the nondrawing arm. The large paper helps them to feel that they have more room to draw.

Give each student a half stick of compressed charcoal and a large piece of paper. Each student should find a starting point and draw that shape on the paper. They draw only around the outside outlines of the chairs and stools, which includes drawing the inner space of the back of the chair or inside the rungs or steps of the ladder or between the wooden or metal rungs on the stool.

Think about this kind of drawing as an add on process. In the sense that you draw one area, leave the positive area the white of the paper and draw the next negative area on the other side. In this way the students add one shape onto the next. If they draw one inner space on the ladder, they then leave the space of the step on the paper and draw the next empty space on the other side. They can move up one side of the ladder this way, leaving the space of the wooden or aluminum side and then draw down the other side.

Concentration is important because it is so easy to lose your place. If students do, they can find another starting spot and start again. It is helpful to fill the empty space in with a solid black to help keep track of where you are in the drawing.

SUPPLIES

1. 18" x 24" white paper

2. Half stick compressed charcoal

3. Hand rags or tissues

Fill the paper top to bottom and running off one of the sides. Blacken all negative space and leave all positive space the white of the paper. The compressed charcoal will get darker and richer if it is rubbed into the paper with a bare finger or tissue around the finger. The small, square size of the charcoal is helpful during the drawing as it allows the students to twist and turn around shapes, shading an area while drawing it.

GOALS

This is a demanding visual exercise that improves the students' understanding of space. It improves decision-making skills and hand-eye coordination.

Drawing I, College Student, Negative Space, Charcoal.

SUMMARY OF STEPS

1. Stack up chairs, stools, or stepladders.
2. Give students large sheets of paper.
3. Ask the students to draw only negative spaces.
4. Find a starting space.
5. Draw the outline of a negative space and fill it in with charcoal.
6. Add a second empty space.
7. Leave the positive spaces white.
8. Blacken in all negative spaces from top to bottom.
9. Rub the charcoal for a deep black.

Samantha Polfus, Grade 4, Continuous Ink Line Drawing

INK AND CONTINUOUS LINE: BALANCING POSITIVE AND NEGATIVE SPACE

BRIEF OVERVIEW

This exercise is an extension of the Continuous Line exercise in Section One. It provides an opportunity for students to experiment with the process of ink line drawing. The tool they will use is a non-free-flowing instrument, a stick. Any stick may be used. Little branches off a bamboo stock work extremely well but twigs from oak, elm, birch, or any native deciduous tree will work.

The line will be irregular, uneven and blotchy, and that is the correct character for the line in this exercise. As in Continuous Line I, the line wraps around, across, over and in between the objects in the still life. The line will cross itself many times in order to move from one form to another. Except for lifting the stick to refill the point, the stick should never leave the paper and the line should be continuous. After the student dips the stick in the ink, the stick is placed back on the drawing where he or she ran out of ink and the drawing continues.

The students may help prepare for this exercise by looking for small twigs on the ground on their way to and from school. To collect still life objects have the students bring them from home—something from their garage, kitchen, or bedroom. Tell them to be sure to ask their parents if they may take these things to school.

THE SETUP

Randomly place many objects down a long table, setting them three or four deep across the table. The students then sit on both sides of the table. If the classroom space is too small, try two or three setups around the room. Each student will need access to a small dish or bottle of ink. They will use a round or quill brush, a stick, and a piece of tag board.

The drawing of the objects in the still life should cover the paper from side to side and from top to bottom in one continuous line. If the students start on the left side of their paper working front to back they should steadily move to the right side of the paper. They start the drawing by selecting an object that is located in the still life on their left; then fill the page with the remaining objects located to their right in the still life. They should continue to draw objects until they run out of paper side to side and top to bottom.

Don't rush through the drawing. Ask them to take time looking at each shape they are drawing, and looking at what object is next. They will need to consider which direction to go, and which object to draw next. To get from one object to the next they draw a line across the paper from one object to the other. This line corresponds to the negative space they are visually crossing on the table. They may backtrack if they miss something they want to include, and the line may cross the object's surface from side to side as well as shaping the object's outline.

The line defines the object, the ground, and the empty space between objects. The ground is the table and the background; anything they can see can be included in this drawing.

To start, they dip the stick in the ink and test it on a piece of scrap paper. Once they get it flowing with the first dip and a mark-making test it will flow more easily. The line should follow the outside and then the inside shape of the first object and then slide across the space of the paper that represents the table—continuing uninterrupted around and across the next object.

The students do not have to stay on the outline of the object, they may draw a line that crosses the surface of the vase or bottle to get to the other side. Lines that are drawn on the surface may be there for many reasons:

SUPPLIES

1. 12" X 18" tag board
2. Small jar or dish of ink
3. Round or quill brush
4. Stick
5. Piece of scrap paper
6. Rag or paper towel

1. To follow some surface change like a label or ridge or metal band

2. To follow a light change

3. To indicate there is a solid surface

4. As a solution for getting from one side of the form to the other

Once they have filled the page with overlapping lines they move to the second phase. Ask the students to search through their drawing for the smallest shapes that were created when lines overlapped and crossed. Using their paint brushes dipped in ink they fill the areas in as solid black.

The small spaces may be in the positive space, or the negative or empty space of the drawing. Filling them in provides the students with a new perspective on their drawing. The black solid shapes now compete with the large outlines of the forms, forcing the eye to bounce around the drawing. This also gives the drawing a certain quality of abstraction.

Boy Drawing, Glencoe School, Portland, Oregon

In a drawing, if all lines are the same weight—the same thickness, or thinness—it visually flattens the drawing. When different shapes are created in dark values the eye can move around the drawing much more easily. Line differences make drawings more appealing and more spatial.

GOALS

This exercise improves the students' hand-eye coordination—developing their awareness of how to translate three-dimensional space into two-dimensional space. The final drawing looks more abstract than realistic, demonstrating one process of working abstractly to the students. They are first practicing using ink and then understanding the technique for working with ink.

In addition, this is one way to explain the importance of positive and negative space. The objects, when no longer separated from the empty space and the ground around them, take on a different sense. The positive space of the object is now mixed up with the negative space—the empty space around and between the objects.

SUMMARY OF STEPS

1. Pick a starting place in the still life.
2. Dip the stick in the ink.
3. Follow the outline of the object.
4. Keep the stick on the paper, using a continuous line.
5. Draw a line from the first object to the next across the paper.
6. Move from left to right and front to back, filling the paper.
7. Draw around and across the objects.
8. Cover the paper with one continuous line crisscrossing itself.
9. Run off two or three edges of the paper.
10. Fill in small sections of the drawing with black ink.

Jean Dubuffet, French 1901–1985, *Memoration XII*, pen and ink on paper with collage, 1978, 51 x 70 cm. Restricted gift of the Print and Drawing Club Fund, 1979.285. Photograph © 1995, The Art Institute of Chicago. All rights reserved.

SHAPE AND SPACE: A COLLAGE

BRIEF OVERVIEW

The shape of the object defines it for us. A shape is two-dimensional, having only height and width. There are two basic categories of shapes—geometric and organic. Geometric shapes may be created by mathematical laws. Geometric shapes are squares, rectangles, triangles, pentagons, hexagons, and trapezoids as well as circles, ovals, and ellipses.

Organic shapes tend to be round and are most often found in nature. The outline of the amoeba is soft and curvy—rather free flowing. People are made up of organic shapes, as are flowers, vines, trees, and fruits. Organic shapes are soft, round, and flowing as opposed to the angular, stiff, or rigid geometric shapes.

In this exercise the students balance organic shapes with geometric shapes filling the positive and negative spaces in their compositions. A combination of materials may be used, including pencil, charcoal, and ink along with an assortment of materials. Possible choices of materials are newspapers, wallpaper samples, painted papers, magazine photos, or fabrics in addition to the drawing tools.

For painted papers, have the students paint sheets of paper with tempera or watercolor the day before you do this exercise. Tempera tends to flake off paper but by adding a tablespoon of acrylic matte medium to one cup of tempera paint it becomes pliable and elastic, eliminating the cracking problem.

Romare Bearden, American, 1914–1988, *The Return of Odysseus (Homage to Pintoricchio and Benin)*, collage on hardboard, 1977, 112 x 142 cm. Mary and Leigh Block Fund for Acquisitions, 1977.127. Photograph © 1995, The Art Institute of Chicago. All rights reserved.

THE SETUP

Select a focus or subject for the collage—perhaps something from the history lessons you are studying. Romare Bearden titled his collage *The Return of Odysseus (Homage to Pentoricchio and Benin),* on the previous page. In this way he directs our focus to a particular subject. Select animals or people and a place, space, or location for them to be placed.

The 18-inch x 24-inch paper covers the student's desk entirely. Thus, it may be helpful to arrange the students in a circle with an empty desk in the middle on which they can place their supplies, and collage materials.

Start by mapping out on the paper, approximately the size each figure will be and where they will be, then sketch in the background loosely. Things will change in construction. The figures may be out of proportion. It is often easier to construct a figure by cutting out the head, body, arms, and legs and gluing them together than it is to draw them.

The students may select any material to cut the shapes out of for their collages. They may cut out the head and add the arm and then the body all out of different materials. They should assemble the parts. They can use ink, charcoal, or pencil to fill in areas. They may make patterns or textures in the background or on the figures.

The organic shapes of the figures should be balanced against geometric shapes in the background. If they have a shape glued down and they need to put something behind it they may use tracing paper to trace the shape. The tracing will give them the actual size of the shape to be made. To transfer a tracing , shade the back of the paper with a 6B pencil. Use the side of the lead and rub it gently across the back of the line areas. The 6B pencil is soft and black, making a perfect carbon surface. Then trace the shape on the material to be used by lying the outlined shape on top of the material and drawing along the traced lines.

SUPPLIES

1. 18" x 24" tag board
2. 6B, HB pencils
3. Ink, pen, sticks or brush
4. Charcoal, vine and compressed
5. Collage materials
6. Tracing paper
7. Glue

To build this composition it is easiest to work from the background to the foreground. Placing all the background shapes on first allows the students to then stack the foreground shapes on top of them; however, sometimes they will need to work back and forth between the two areas, as they won't always know what they want to do until they do it. Each addition changes the composition. The students should feel free to work over areas and to work back and forth in the composition.

GOALS

The students must plan their compositions and decide on the placement of each part. They must select their own materials. Decision-making skills are developed and critical thinking is mandatory. They will learn by doing and discover that an initial plan may have to be changed along the way. They must regroup throughout this process.

SUMMARY OF STEPS

1. Pick a subject for the collage.
2. Map out the figures and the background lightly.
3. Select materials to use.
4. Cut out shapes and paste them down.
5. Use charcoal or ink in areas.
6. Balance the organic shapes with the geometric.
7. Encourage students to change things as they work.
8. Use tracings to fit shapes around shapes.

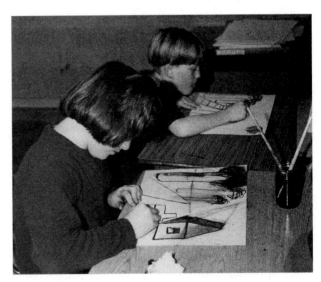

Bonnie Pierce and Andrew Rowlett Share Supplies at Glencoe School, Portland, Oregon

William T. Wiley, *Portrait of Apollinaire, (Ooga),* 1965, mixed media on paper, 11" x 13" (27.9 x 33.0 cm).
San Francisco Museum of Modern Art. Gift of Dr. and Mrs. William R. Fielder, 86.126.

VALUE CREATES SPACE: WORKING LIGHT TO DARK

BRIEF OVERVIEW

There is no single way to indicate space. Artists may comply with nature to describe space by rendering natural light, or they can promote the feeling of space by the use of value. One approach to depicting space is to use a progression of values from front to back, or side to side, moving from light to dark. Another is the reverse, in which the foreground is dark and the background is light. Perspective and value can combine to create a deep sense of space. This drawing exercise focuses on three distinct levels of space: foreground, middle ground, and background. The process may help students to understand where and how to place what they are seeing onto the paper. William Wiley's drawing on the facing page is constructed in three sections moving from light to dark.

The following exercises may be helpful to do before this one, Warm-up for Ink Drawing, Outline Drawing, and Cylinder Study.

THE SETUP

SUPPLIES

1. 12" x 18" tag board
2. HB pencil
3. Sumi ink
4. Brush
5. Pen
6. Water
7. Three small jars or dishes

Set up a subject to draw that has three large areas—for example, a large plant beside a window with a bike outside the window; or a chair, a lamp, and a wall with pictures on it; or the plant, a ladder, and a suitcase placed upright. Use large objects placed in a horizontal line to be divided into three big flat spaces. A piece of plaid or striped fabric can be placed under or behind one of the objects to add pattern to the drawing.

Start with the HB pencil and have the students make a light outline of the three subjects, dividing the drawing into three sections. Prepare the first two dishes or jars of ink wash. In the first one put straight sumi ink, and in the second jar make up a wash of 1/4 C. water with two drops of ink. Two or three students can share one setup by arranging their desks close to each other.

When the students finish their outlines of the objects placed side by side across the paper, start with the first wash placing it over the middle and the left sections. Let them dry. A third jar is needed to hold clean water to rinse the brush and pen out.

Dip the pen in the sumi ink and outline the objects in the first part of the drawing on the right of the page. The first object is left in outline without a wash on it. The students may use the brush and pen to texturize areas in this first area.

Return to the middle section and outline the shapes over the wash. Outline the shapes in the third section on the left also. Darken the wash mixture and put another wash over the far left section.

Now balance the composition with more line or more wash to achieve a three-part drawing in which section one on the right is white in outline, the middle ground is gray with a black outline, and the left section is the darkest area. This arrangement of values should force the object on the right to appear in front of the other two and thus closest to the viewer. The dark area should seem furthest away.

Richard Diebenkorn on the facing page is as masterful as Goya in the use of light and dark values throughout his drawing. Notice how he moves the eye from one shape on the figure to the shape in the room next to it and back to the figure. The whole drawing is beautifully balanced from light to dark and from foreground to background.

GOALS

To help the students understand how value change from light to dark and front to back creates space. Students practice layering ink wash and line. They must judge the relative lightness and darkness of the areas in their drawings. The drawings must be planned and using critical thinking and decision-making skills.

SUMMARY OF STEPS

1. Divide the drawing in three sections.
2. Draw outline of three objects with the HB pencil lightly.
3. Make a medium gray wash.
4. Wash over middle and left sections.
5. Let the wash dry.
6. Outline right section in ink line.
7. Outline objects in middle section.
8. Wash over the far left section again.
9. Balance drawing with more line or wash.
10. Add texture and pattern.
11. Right section is white with ink outline.
12. Middle section is gray with outline.
13. Left side is now dark with dark outline.

Richard Diebenkorn, *Seated Figure from the Portfolio, Ten West Coast Artists,* 1967, lithograph, Collectors Press 9/75, image 29 1/4" x 22 3/8". San Francisco Museum of Modern Art. Gift of Spaulding Taylor, 82.481.3.

Johannes Bosboom, Dutch 1817–1891, *Church Interior,* watercolor and gouache over graphite on cream laid paper, n.d., 41 x 31.2 cm. Bequest of Irving K. Pond, 1939.2243. Photograph © 1995, The Art Institute of Chicago. All rights reserved.

SPACE AND SCALE

BRIEF OVERVIEW

In Johannes Bosboom's *Church Interior* on the facing page, the scale of the church overwhelms the people seen in the back; the people look like mice. By altering the spatial relationship of the church to the people, in which he makes the church look huge and the people look tiny, the artist creates a sense of an enormous space. We can see it; we feel we are looking deep into a long church hallway, and far away from us stand the people talking. Artists can create space by changing the scale and proportions of a room to the people or objects in it.

The exercise for One-point Perspective is necessary to do prior to doing this exercise. The exercise, Value Creates Space, would also be helpful to do prior to doing this one.

THE SETUP

Place a small table or stool with three items on it, sitting on a piece of white paper, in front of the windows. Use a bottle, a grapefruit, and a vase or a pitcher, a jug, and a large book. Arrange the students as far away from the table as possible. It may be wise to set up five such still lifes along the windows and put five or six students in front of each one. Try to keep the students sitting directly in front of the still life so they have as much of a frontal view as possible. If you don't have windows, use a long wall in the room and hang three narrow pieces of cloth behind each table. Sheets divided into long strips will work fine.

The students may draw on boards held on their laps or, if there's room, place their desks in front of them. Each student starts by locating the horizon line, which they know to be their eye level. Draw the horizon line on the paper.

Next draw a rectangle receding for the top of the table, and draw it vanishing to the horizon. This table top may also be referred to as a plane. Locate the vanishing point (VP). Add the legs by drawing a line to the VP from the bottom of the front legs. Draw a vertical line for the legs between the top of the table and this bottom line.

SUPPLIES

1. 12" x 18" white paper
2. HB, 3B pencils
3. Ruler
4. Compressed charcoal
5. Water
6. Brush
7. Plastic eraser
8. Drawing boards (optional)

Draw the outline of the objects on top of the table. Look at the windows or fabric in the background and draw lines from the top of the paper to where they intersect the table and the objects. Draw as many lines as needed to define divisions in the background.

To draw the floor in perspective, locate the vanishing point for the table top. Mark it on the horizon. Using a ruler at the bottom edge of the paper, measure off one-inch units. Then draw a receding diagonal line from each one-inch mark to the vanishing point on the horizon (see Diagram III). Draw a horizontal line for where the floor ends behind the table. Now draw a diagonal line from the right back corner (Point A to B in Diagram III) to the front left corner. Take the ruler and draw horizontal lines at the points where the A/B diagonal line intersects each diagonal line receding from the bottom edge of the paper. This makes a grid for the floor which puts it in perspective. Notice that each row of squares gets smaller as they get closer to the horizon.

Diagram I

Diagram II

To make it look like a tile floor, blacken every other tile in the grid accenting the sense of moving back in space. Blacken the windows and the area behind the table, then pick and choose light and dark values for the rest of the drawing. Compressed charcoal can be turned into a wash with water. If an area has been covered with charcoal and the students run a wet brush over it, the brush will pick up some of the charcoal and that gray can be used in other parts of the drawing. A scrap piece of tag

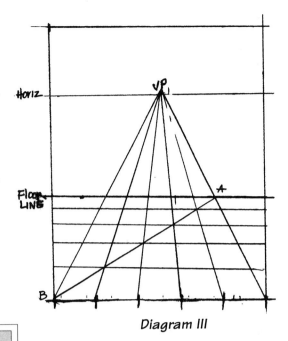

Diagram III

SUMMARY OF STEPS

1. Set up a still life at the far end of the room.
2. Set the students directly in front of the still life.
3. Draw the horizon line on the paper.
4. Draw the table top with lines to VP on horizon.
5. Draw lines to VP from the bottom of the front table leg.
6. Draw the outlines of the objects.
7. Draw lines to define fabric or windows in background.
8. Mark off 1" units on front edge of paper.
9. Draw floor lines receding to VP from front edge.
10. Draw a horizontal line for back floor line.
11. Draw a diagonal from back to front.
12. Draw horizontal lines at intersections of the diagonal and the receding floor lines.
13. Blacken in every other square on the floor.
14. Select values for the rest of the drawing.
15. Use compressed charcoal as a wash.

board may be used to hold compressed charcoal for the brush to be wiped through to create values. Keep the brush damp, tipping it in water as you work.

The floor and the back wall or windows should dwarf the table. Now the table seems small and the room seems large.

GOALS

To show the students how to manipulate the space of a drawing by using a scale change. To improve their understanding of perspective. This exercise increases decision-making skills. The students combine an understanding of balancing value with perspective throughout the drawing.

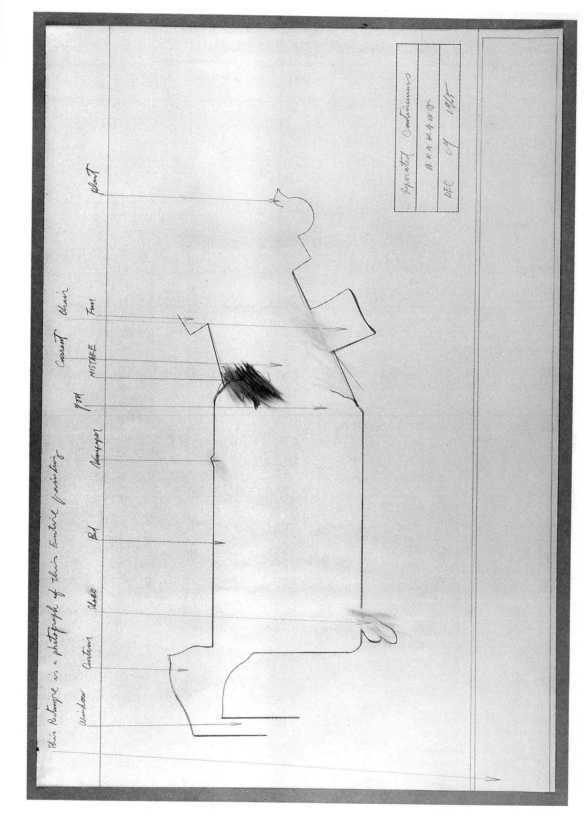

CONTINUOUS ROOM DRAWING

BRIEF OVERVIEW

This drawing takes in the entire room. The students must consider how to get the outline shape of the entire space of the room on the paper in one continuous line.

THE SETUP

Each student starts by taking a long look around the perimeter of the room. Only the top outline of the chairs, tables, and objects sitting along the windows will be included in this drawing. Using a black felt-tip or roller-ball pen and white paper, pick a starting point and very slowly construct a line around the perimeter of the room moving from shape to shape. Try to get the entire room in an outline around the edges of the paper. The students will have to turn their gaze and rotate their papers to follow their outline around the room. Ask them not to rush, but to take time really trying to render each individual shape they see. Everyone may pick a separate line.

At one point in the drawing they are to enter the center of the paper on the left or right and construct one small space from the center of the room. They could also draw one part of an object in the room.

There is no erasing but they may use more than one line if they need to. If a line is not where it should be just stop and reposition the pen to start again. Every mark or line they make only improves the drawing and makes it more individual. Each line is a record of what they were thinking and seeing.

Samantha Polfus, Grade 4, Continuous Line Drawing, Ink

GOALS

To develop better visual translating skills. To improve hand-eye coordination and build confidence in the students about their ability to draw. Everyone succeeds with this drawing.

SUMMARY OF STEPS

1. Look around the perimeter of the room.
2. Examine the tops of the shapes around the room.
3. Very slowly begin a line formed by those shapes.
4. Follow the top shapes around the room.
5. Turn the paper.
6. Students should turn their heads to look.
7. Come into the center of the paper at one point.
8. Draw one contour detail in the room.

DRAWING INTERIOR SPACE: GIACOMETTI STYLE

BRIEF OVERVIEW

The exercises on one- and two-point perspective are helpful to do prior to this exercise. In this exercise the students discover how to translate the space of the room onto a flat piece of paper by considering the relationship of one form to another. The height and width of each form or object to be included in the drawing is decided by comparing them with a standard of measurement—the lone chair in the middle of the room. The students will look at the space in the room, finding and adding each object or form one by one.

The paper will be covered with lines. No erasing is ever necessary, as a line placed in error is replaced by another line and they can just ignore the first line. The first lines drawn should be drawn lightly.

Since their desks take up so much space, an alternative arrangement is to have them sit in their chairs with a drawing board on their laps. Any hard surface as big as their paper will do for a drawing board. Sheets of masonite at hardware stores can cost as little as $2.00 and they are big enough to be divided into four to six boards. Composition board is cheap or you can use a piece of stiff cardboard.

In this drawing the students construct the interior space by finding where every object is in terms of the chair or stool sitting in the middle of the space. All other forms in the room are placed according to how much taller or shorter they are than the chair or the stool. All the furniture in the room is drawn according to how far it is from the chair. The students may sit anywhere in the room where they have a clear view of the chair.

The example by Giacometti shows how he uses this loose line drawing to establish the space he is drawing. By relating one object to others, the students can get a better sense of space and proportion in their drawings . Students tend to miniaturize space. They look at one object, draw it, and then make all other objects in the room small in order to fit them into the drawing. This exercise can change their perception and understanding of space.

GIACOMETTI, Alberto. *The Artist's Mother*, 1950. Oil on canvas, 35 3/8" x 24". The Museum of Modern Art, New York. Acquired through the Lillie P. Bliss Bequest. Photograph © 1995 The Museum of Modern Art, New York.

THE SETUP

Put the students at either end of the classroom, sitting zigzagged so they can all see the middle and opposite end of the room. They can sit in their chairs with the drawing boards on their laps. Start with the HB pencil.

Place a stool or chair in the middle of the room. This is the standard by which all else will be measured. Establish the horizon line at eye level then begin the drawing with an outline of the chair or stool. Locate the chair on the paper with a horizon line and place the chair to the left or the right of the center of the paper, depending on each student's view.

The students looking at the stool from the right side of the room may place it on the left side of their paper. If they are looking from the left side of the room, the stool may be placed more to the right side of their paper. The drawing of the chair can be just a few vertical and horizontal lines. Volume is achieved in this drawing by continuing to add overlapping lines that become forms.

The students will draw lines from the chair across the floor to the next object on the left and then draw lines to the objects on the right. Their lines construct the height of the objects on the left and the right by comparing them with the height of the chair in the middle. Continue locating everything else in the room with lines

Diagram I: Establish Space with Vertical and Horizontal Lines.

Diagram II: Locate Vanishing Lines to One Point or Two Points, Depending on Student's Angle.

drawn across the empty space to where all other objects sit.

To judge the distance between objects, draw a line across the floor to another object, then compare the distance to the size of the chair. Should that distance be the same as the chair, smaller than the chair, twice as far as the size of the chair? The students must interpret the space of the room to the space of the paper.

Draw a line from the base of the chair to where it intersects whatever is on the right side. Sketch in a vertical line to establish the front edge of whatever is there. It could be a cabinet or desk. Rather than drawing outlines, draw lines for where a form starts, for how tall and how wide it is.

Repeat for objects to the left. The lines for the top of, say, a table will vanish to the back of the room as a diagonal line receding and slightly angling in and up toward the horizon of the room. The one-point exercise in perspective can help the students understand this a bit better.

Continue drawing lines from all sections of the chair; draw from the top of the back of the chair, from the front and back legs of the chair, and from the seat. Locate the objects in the room by drawing lines from the chair across the empty space. Overlapping and layering lines will create a sense of volume.

The lines will go horizontally, vertically, and diagonally around the room, crossing the distance on the paper that will indicate the amount of space between the chair and the desk or the cabinet or the table or the windows.

The line is not an outline but a unit of measurement. When the students are deciding how to show the space behind the chair, have them look at where the top of the chair is in terms of the cabinet behind it. Consider the size of the cabinet from the top of the chair. Is it shorter than the top of the chair or taller? Then draw a line to indicate the distance.

They should not be thinking about how big they know the cabinet is but how much of the object behind the chair they actually see, without moving their heads. They can attempt to include the ceiling with a few marks if they like.

Draw lightly at first to establish the

Diagram III

space. Then switch to a darker pencil like the 3B pencil to reinforce areas when they feel they have the proper placement. Don't outline any objects; leave them unconstructed and formed only by the overlapping lines.

FELT-TIP PEN OPTION

The students may also make this drawing with a black felt pen. With the felt pen they realize in advance there will be no erasing. Sometimes using the felt pen first relaxes the students so they cease to worry about the right and wrong of line placement. Then the next day you can do the same problem using pencils.

This exercise should be repeated to build their skills; they learn something new each time they do an exercise. This may even surprise them, as they are so used to the idea that we do something once and then move to the next level.

Artists spend years drawing the same model or space over and over to develop an awareness and an understanding of form or space. Zen artists of Japan have been known to draw a chrysanthemum every day for ten years to perfect their understanding of the form. An artist may make a stack of drawings over a couple of weeks to work out an idea. The first study of any subject will be vague; only with repeated drawings will the initially unnoticed details reveal themselves.

SUMMARY OF STEPS

1. Set a chair at the end of the room.
2. Set the students at the opposite end of the room.
3. Use pen or pencils on paper
4. Give students drawing boards.
5. Map out the chair first with vertical and horizontal lines.
6. Draw the room by comparing each object with the chair.
7. Determine the height of the other objects by measuring them against the chair.
8. Use a line to show the distance other things are from the chair.
9. Draw lines across empty space from one object to another.
10. Draw the space behind the chair.

GOALS

Translating space is not something we come by naturally. We learn to visualize space. This drawing process develops our ability to see and draw a space in perspective. To draw, we must forget what we know and draw what we see. For example, we know a desk is larger than a stool, but it won't be if the desk is farther away from our drawing point of view. Objects in the foreground will be bigger than the objects in the background. Objects and forms in perspective seem smaller as they get further away from us. This exercise helps students to put space in perspective.

Jack Beal, American, b. 1931, *Sleeping Bag and Pillow*, charcoal on white wove paper, 1967, 48 x 65.5 cm., Gift of Frank Hubacheck, 1968.41. Photograph © 1995, The Art Institute of Chicago. All rights reserved.

DRAWING DRAPERY

BRIEF OVERVIEW

Drapery is difficult to draw because there are no outlines to follow. To draw drapery the students must divide the flowing or folded surface into planes. The students will use value changes to separate the planes. They must move from white to gray to black. Sometimes you can see the places where the light changes across the form, but often the artist must decide where the breaks are to create the sense of drapery as a sculptural form.

Jack Beal's *Sleeping Bag and Pillow* on the facing page uses value change to achieve a feeling of volume in this pile of fabric. Striped fabric is helpful to draw, by following the stripes the students can form the surface. Notice how the stripes are offset; when they turn into a crease they come up on top of the next fold a little to the left or right.

THE SETUP

To practice finding the planes on a draped piece of fabric, follow the steps in the diagram. Notice the folds of the drapery in the example are referred to as side planes, top plane, and back plane. To practice making the basic form of drapery, draw a wavy line on the bottom of the page, then make two marks on either side of each top wave. Place a single point on the paper six inches above the wavy line. This point is called a hub. Draw a line from the two points on top of the waves to the hub (Diagram I).

To find the sides of the fold, make two lines on either side of each lower wave and mark those with dots. Draw lines to the hub from these marks. Then draw a line from the

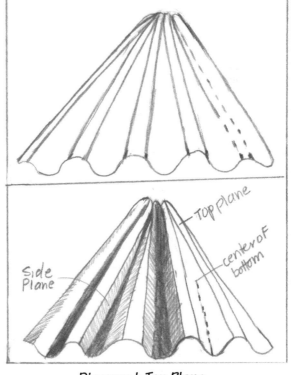

Diagram I: Top Plane
Diagram II: Top and Side Planes

center of the lower wave to the hub (Diagram II). To shape these lines into a flowing drapery, leave the top plane white and use a gray value on each side with a dark or black value in the center area of the lower curve.

Vine charcoal is very soft and easy to manipulate. Use the vine charcoal first on the back plane. The back plane is the part of the fabric that is indented and closest to the wall or table the drapery is placed on. The stump or a tissue is then wiped into the charcoal, picking up some of the black on the end, to create the gray on the sides of the fold. We use the stump because it applies value without making hard edges. The stump is easier to control than direct use of charcoal. It will make a light gray, as it is not saturated with charcoal and allows the student to gradually build up the surface. The back plane will need another layer of charcoal to darken it down.

The stump may be cleaned by scraping off the dirty end with a pencil sharpener or knife; a mat knife may be used. The scraping in the same motion used in sharpening a pencil by hand with a knife. The kneaded eraser may be used to lift out charcoal and smudges.

Test the students' understanding of this formula for drawing drapery with the following exercise. Hang a white bed sheet from a tack on the wall and let it flare out at the bottom. Form the drapery by pinning it in place at the bottom. A light on the hanging drape can help the students see the changes across the form. If you have a lamp or a floodlight, place it on one side.

One way to think of how drapery falls is to think of it as having a top, two sides, and a background. The top surface or plane is closest to the light, the background is the part of the sheet that is touching the wall it is hanging on and furtherest away. The sides are the areas of the fold that turn back from the top to the back plane. In this first study, the top plane should be white, the sides should be gray and the back plane should be black.

Sometimes the fold will be so severe that the light of the top surface will fold immediately into the dark of the back-

Diagram III

Drawing I, University Student, Drapery Study

ground without a gray side between them. Sometimes the drapery will have a long span in the background that is gray with creases of black across it. It is necessary to consider the balance of black, white, and gray values in creating the illusion of form flowing and moving up and down across a surface.

GOALS

To develop skill in drawing fabric. The students must make decisions for placing divisions that will sculpt the fabric. Critical thinking must work with seeing to accomplish this task. Interpretive skills are necessary to draw drapery.

SUMMARY OF STEPS

1. Draw a wavy line. Place a point 6" above it.
2. Draw a line from either side of the top curve to the hub which is the point.
3. Draw a line from the center of the lower curve to the hub.
4. Draw two lines from either side of the lower curve.
5. Use value to form drapery.
6. The top plane is left white.
7. Blacken the back plane in the middle of the lower wave.
8. Wipe the stump into the charcoal on the back plane.
9. Use dirty stump to make gray sides.
10. Add more charcoal to back plane.
11. Try the process looking at a real drapery.

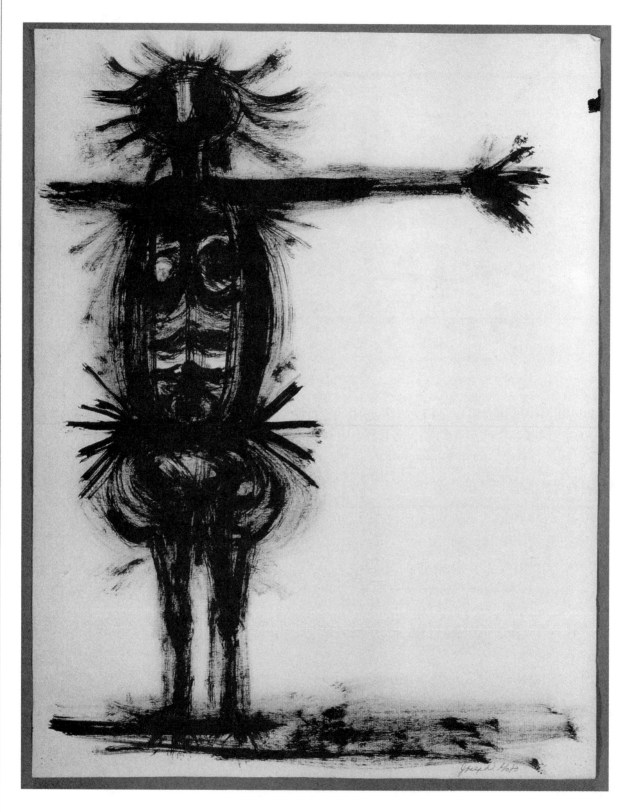

Joseph Goto, American, 1915–1994, *Untitled (Single Figure)*, brush and black ink on cream laid paper, n.d., 63.8 x 43.4 cm. Gift of Mr. and Mrs. Joseph R. Shapiro, 1992.229. Photograph © 1995, The Art Institute of Chicago. All rights reserved.

SECTION FIVE:
Texture

TEXTURE INTRODUCTION

BRIEF OVERVIEW

Texture in drawing represents the relationship between sight and touch. We can imagine how a surface feels by looking at it and vice versa we can imagine how a surface looks by touching it.

In the Renaissance the ideal was that a painting should be a "window into space." A smooth surface with no recognizable brush strokes; no surface textures were to interfere with the spatial illusion. In the middle of the nineteenth century the Impressionists opened the doors to radical change in the attitude toward surface texture. Art was released from its duty to create only spatial illusion. Painters used the brush stroke not only to interpret the textural qualities of the surface but to represent light and space.

The twentieth century continued the revolution, first with the Cubists who introduced collage—adding not only flat papers to their work but also materials like sand, physically altering the surface. The technique of assemblage followed collage in which dimensional materials were added creating high or low relief. The Dadaists invented photomontage—combining photographs with letter forms. More recently, photocopying has enhanced this process. Currently art is wide open to an expressive range of material options.

The role of texture in a drawing is varied. Texture can appear to be rough or smooth, or it can actually be rough or smooth to the touch. The surface can be coarse or glossy, soft or hard. The actual texture of the surface can contribute to the type of texture created, or a specific tool may be invented to create a texture. Texture can be used in a drawing to represent a known surface or textures may be invented to serve the drawing abstractly.

THE SETUP

The textures in this exercise are invented. The students will make them up out of their imaginations. The Outline Drawing exercise would be helpful to do prior to this one. The subject is an overstuffed chair or armchair. If you have one in your room, the students can draw it. If not, cut some photos out of *Architectural Digest* to use as subjects, or have the students take a piece of paper home and sketch the outline of a chair in their own living rooms.

Each student is to make a large contour or outline drawing of the shape of the chair. They do not need to draw any arm or pillow or seat details. They may indicate where those separations are if they want to but they don't have to.

Once they have a pencil outline, they divide the outline arbitrarily, or by the divisions they noted between the arm and seat, seat and back, and so on. Then in each divided section, they invent a texture for the area with colored markers. Surround each of the colored sections with a thick black line. They can mix colors or change colors— whatever they choose. The color choice is up to the student.

I have suggested a square piece of paper because it will give them more spatial options, but they can use a rectangle if you prefer.

Mount the drawing on black construction paper to accent the colored marker.

211

Jessica Pliskin, Grade 4, Textured Trees

GOALS

To enhance creative and inventive thinking. To improve hand-eye coordination skills. To encourage the students to make individual decisions in the development of their drawing.

SUMMARY OF STEPS

1. Select an armchair for the subject.
2. Draw a large outline.
3. Divide the interior space arbitrarily or by the design of the chair.
4. Fill each division with invented texture marks.
5. Mount on black paper.

Jean Dubuffet, French, 1901–1985, *Untitled,* colored marker on paper, 1966, 28.4 x 21.6 cm. Bequest of Soloman B. Smith, 1986.1601. Photograph © 1995, The Art Institute of Chicago. All rights reserved.

TEXTURED ROOM

BRIEF OVERVIEW

Texture, whether it is real, imitated from nature, or invented adds a special quality to a drawing. It announces space where there is none. It creates surface and a certain visual excitement for the eye.

A heavily textured drawing like Simon Dinnerstein's is a feast for the eyes. You can't stop looking around this drawing, and everywhere you look there is an inviting texture that peaks your curiosity and holds your interest.

THE SETUP

The students should do the exercises on Warm-up for Pencil Drawing, Warm-up for Ink Drawing, Building Ink Washes, One-point Perspective, and Two-point Perspective before attempting this one. They will need some technical skills behind them.

Arrange the room so a group of students can sit and look straight on at a wall with a table and chair in front of it—or use any furniture you have in the room for the focus of the drawing. If the wall is a normal institutional wall, it should be altered. You may hang a bedspread across it, or put up fabric or paper it with contact paper. Hang some pictures, a calendar or a mirror on the wall. If the chair is a stiff school chair put two pillows on it, one on the seat, one on the back and cover it with a throw or piece of fabric. You could also take a coat that is striped or flowered and hang it over the back of a chair with the back facing the students. Cardboard boxes, bookcases, or the wall with the sink on it may be used in the setup for the drawings.

> ## SUPPLIES
>
> 1. 12" X 18" tag board
> 2. Pen and ink
> 3. HB pencil
> 4. Felt-tip pens (fine tip)
> 5. Water
> 6. Small dish or jar
> 7. Rag for spills

Simon Dinnerstein, *Marie Bilderl*, 1971, charcoal, conté crayon, 41 1/2" x 49 1/2". Minnesota Museum of Art, Saint Paul, Minnesota.

Start the drawing with the HB pencil and let the students map out the scene. They don't have to map out the textures, just the outline of the furniture to be included in their drawings. Using pen and ink, the students create the textures they see on the wall, the floor, the chair, and so forth. They may imitate a texture or invent a texture for the space if there isn't one there. Have them cover the entire drawing with various marks, stripes, curves, dots, or wood grain imitations. When the drawing is dry, have them mix a wash with water and a few drops of ink and then put the wash on the areas that have shadows, or are under and behind forms, or need to be darkened for contrast in the drawing.

This drawing may take two to three days to complete because it is labor intensive.

GOALS

For students to understand the amount of work that goes into a drawing by this firsthand experience. They must keep their ideas and intentions for the drawing in mind for two or three days. This exercise improves visual memory and depends on continuous decision-making skills.

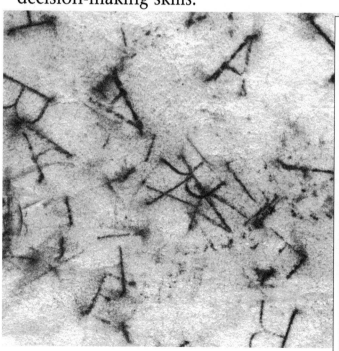

SUMMARY OF STEPS

1. Students should have done recommended exercises previously.
2. Arrange furniture and fabric grouping for students to draw.
3. With the HB pencils students map out the outlines of the objects.
4. Using pen and ink they texture the entire drawing (fine felt-tip pens are an option).
5. When the line drawing is dry, use a wash for value changes.
6 It may take two to three days to finish.

Arshile Gorky, American, b. Armenia, 1904–1948, *Three Forms*, pen and brush with black ink, over pencil with touches of oil paint on paper, 1937, 55 x 72 cm., Grant S. Pick Memorial Fund, 1968.35. Photograph © 1995. The Art Institute of Chicago. All rights reserved.

VAN GOGH'S LANDSCAPE

BRIEF OVERVIEW

Vincent van Gogh was one of the most productive and expressive artists of the nineteenth century. Very few artists today could compete with his productivity. During the fifteen months he lived in Arles in the south of France, he produced some 200 paintings, made over 100 drawings and watercolors, and wrote some 200 letters. Arles was for van Gogh the "land of the blue tones and gay colors."

He created textures and patterns for grass, wind, moving leaves, night light, floors, walls, and stone patios. The direction of the line as well as the length, the balance of the dots and the dashes, and the closeness of each of the lines was all important to him. Each area of the drawing has its own character.

The exercises Warm-up for Ink Drawing, Warm-up for Pencil Drawing, Cross-hatching Practice, Negative Space I and II, and Cylinder Study should be done prior to doing this exercise.

THE SETUP

The students will construct a landscape out of different-sized lines, dots, dashes, circles, ellipses. There can be no outlines of any form or shape. Instead they should use different thick and thin lines for the clouds, air, wind, grasses, leaves, trees, rocks, and buildings.

To start the drawing consider the direction of the line; would a vertical, horizontal, or diagonal be best to interpret the space? Remember to leave spaces between strokes, especially in the trees between the marks for leaves. Consider how many lines each area needs. Should the area be light or dark? Use more overlapping lines in the dark areas. It is necessary to think of both positive and

SUPPLIES

1. Tag board
2. HB pencils
3. Sketch paper
4. Ink and dish
5. Pen and stick
6. Quill brush
7. Fabric
8. Water jar

negative space in the drawing. For example, would you draw the grass or the dark space in the grasses?

For a subject, a field trip with a sketch pad is fun. If you and your students can go on a walk around the block or while you are on a field trip for other reasons, you can take 15 or 30 minutes to sit down and draw the landscape. They will need only a brief sketch of the trees, grass, hills, or buildings. They can return to the classroom with the sketch and use it to develop a landscape.

A second possibility is to make up a landscape or copy van Gogh's. A third possibility is the ever present magazine photo. Nature magazines, *Smithsonian, Life, Travel & Leisure,* and many others now offer beautiful photos of exotic rain forests or countrysides. Perhaps the students could bring in a magazine as an outside assignment to prepare for this drawing.

Tools are important in making marks. You can construct your own tools out of denim, fabrics, and paper. Cut a four-inch to five-inch square of denim out and then roll it up on the diagonal. It will have a penlike tip but it will be floppy. This tool can be dipped in ink and stamped on the paper or whisked across it, or the rough end can be dragged, leaving shaggy marks. Every tool makes a different mark.

GOALS

To develop a surface in a drawing that is built of lines and marks but not outlined. To think of how to interpret the things we see in the landscape in terms of art materials. To decide on tools and how to use them to make appropriate marks.

SUMMARY OF STEPS

1. Discuss Vincent van Gogh's drawing.
2. Make a drawing of the space of a landscape.
3. Or use a photo of a landscape.
4. Select tools to use; make some.
5. Design the landscape with no outlines.
6. Use marks, dots, and dashes to build a landscape.

Rex Amos, American, b. 1935, *The Birth of Creativity*, collage, chiné colle and pastel, 1989,
image 11" x 15", paper size 22 1/4" x 30". Courtesy of the artist and Magnolia Editions, Oakland, CA.

ASSEMBLED DRAWINGS

BRIEF OVERVIEW

This exercise recycles art. So often students are unhappy and disappointed with their work. My friends and I often joke about our failures. Our favorite saying when writing a work off is to say, "Well, it's just not the vision I had!" It is very common in the world of art to start out with a great idea and end up with something completely different from what you expected. Even worse, sometimes one part of the drawing is pleasing, but you can't stand the rest of the drawing. Those drawings end up on the floor or in a box. Each classroom needs such a cardboard box for all rejected drawings, or you can make an individual file for each student to store rejects.

In this exercise you and your students can choose to make the assembled drawing from each student's own drawings or from a big pile of drawings that everyone can choose from. In this way, Rob can use Christian's drawing and John can use Christen's work.

THE SETUP

The students will make a new composition from their old drawings or from classmates' old drawings, as you prefer. They should select three or four drawings that they like something about, and rip or cut out the parts they want to use. If you want a ripped edge, it helps to dampen the crease on the paper where you will rip it. Then the paper pulls apart with a nice soft edge.

SUPPLIES

1. 3B, 6B pencils
2. Old drawings
3. 12" x 18" tag board
4. Ink, brush
5. Plastic erasers
6. Compressed charcoal
7. Glue sticks
8. Small rags

Larry Rivers, American, b. 1923, *The Last Civil War Veteran*, 1961, pencil, black crayon, and paper collage heightened with white gouache on spiral sketch pad sheet; 9 15/16" x 8" (25.2 x 20.3 cm.), sheet. Thomas E. Benesch Memorial Collection, 1961.261. The Baltimore Museum of Art.

Reassemble the selected parts into a new composition on the tag board. The tag board may warp a little if you are using wet glue. It is therefore necessary to press it flat while it dries with weight from books. The students should have a small rag beside them to wipe up any excess glue that leaks out over the edges. Otherwise when you press the collages, the glue will stick to the books and ruin the collage and perhaps the jacket on the book.

After the students have glued the parts together or while they are arranging things, they may add value marks, or gesture marks, or additional drawing elements with pencil or charcoal. They may want to outline parts with ink or pencil or add a texture to an area.

The plastic eraser can be used as a drawing tool. Fill an area with 6B pencil, then use the eraser to rub out some of it, leaving light stripes across the area. When the eraser is dirty, it will also smear areas. An area that has dark pencil marks, when it is erased, will retain the strokes as light marks.

GOALS

This exercise points out to the students that art is a process of constant change. No one drawing is particularly important. A drawing thought to be a failure can be turned into a successful work of art. In art when you think you have failed with a drawing, you also know that you can do another drawing.

SUMMARY OF STEPS

1. Select three or four old drawings.
2. Plan a composition.
3. Pick other materials like pencil to use.
4. Glue sections of drawings with pencil or charcoal together.
5. Outline parts.
6. Add texture with ink to areas.
7. Press the board under weight to flatten.

FAT LANDSCAPE

SUPPLIES

1. 12" x 18" white paper or tag board
2. HB, 3B, and 6B pencils
3. Compressed charcoal
4. Ink and brush
5. Pen
6. Kneaded eraser
7. Plastic eraser

BRIEF OVERVIEW

The Cylinder Study and the Chiaroscuro exercise must be done before attempting this one. Additional exercises, Value Creates Space and Beginning Landscape: One-point Perspective would be helpful as foundations for the students to build on.

Jack Beal's drawing is a wonderful interpretation and extension of landscape. His drawing gives us a new way to view the landscape. He has taken a basically realistic view and enhanced it with his imagination.

THE SETUP

Using the cylinder form, the students will build a landscape out of round tubes. Each tube can be one row in a field. The tree trunks and branches should be formed out of cylinders as well as the houses. Each form in the landscape starts as a large or small cylinder right side up or sideways, and then the students sculpt it into a house, a field, a mountain, or a car.

They may draw whatever they choose in their landscapes. Houses, cars, mountains, fields, trees, clouds, foothills, and walkways are all possibilities—but each part, each form or object of the still life, must start out as a cylinder that can be added on to, repeated, stacked, and finally textured on one side.

The students should map out the drawing in HB pencil, first planning where each part should go. Once they have their plan, they move to the materials they prefer—ink, compressed charcoal, pen, brush, stick, and so on. By now the students should have done lessons with ink and charcoal, and they can choose one or both. They can stay dry or use water and add wash with ink or compressed charcoal.

To keep the feeling of roundness to the landscape, make sure all outside lines curve. The house may be constructed out of two cylinders overlapped and connected as the boxes were in the Perspective I exercise. When students are forming the fields, the front ellipse may be totally cut off by the front edge of the drawing so you see only the curves receding from the edge as Jack Beal has done. In addition, the front ellipse may be large and the back ellipse small to enhance the sense of moving back in space. By overlapping forms one section in the front of the drawing is easily integrated with a form in the back of the drawing. The cylinders may be formed below the horizon or above the horizon.

GOALS

This exercise enhances the students' abilities to translate and interpret information. It combines a number of previously learned exercises with creative thinking and planning. Decision-making skills are further developed through individual choices and expression.

SUMMARY OF STEPS

1. Discuss the Cylinder Study, and One-point Perspective.
2. Discuss what can be included in the drawing.
3. Invent a landscape out of cylinders.
4. Outline drawing with the HB Pencil.
5. Select other materials for texture in the drawing.

CUBIST COLLAGE

BRIEF OVERVIEW

Collage is a work of art made by pasting various scraps or pieces of material—cloth, paper, photographs—onto a surface, creating a new composition. The process of pasting or gluing fragments of printed matter, fabric, natural material or anything that is relatively flat—onto the two-dimensional surface of a canvas or panel is collage. Collage may also be thought of as a very low-relief assemblage. Collage introduces into the space of drawing materials from the everyday world; the world of art collides with the real world.

The collage by Georges Braque on the following page combines charcoal, graphite, oil paint, and watercolor with paper elements in his collage. He imitates real surfaces with drawing and also adds real materials to the collage. Collage is an *inclusive*—not *exclusive*—medium. It admits anything and everything into its world.

THE SETUP

The students must collect a selection of materials. Their compositions will be a balance between real materials and drawn shapes. Materials to collect can be newspapers, wallpaper samples, wood grain contact paper, posters, photos, and fabrics.

For the drawn objects, set single bottles, vases, musical instruments, or fruit bowls around the room—but not in arrangements. Have the students cut pieces of white drawing paper up into sizes that one object can be drawn on. Papers should range from 4" x 6" to 6" x 8". Each drawing should fill the piece of paper it is drawn on from top to bottom.

SUPPLIES

1. White drawing paper
2. HB pencil
3. Real materials
4. 12" x 18" tag board
5. Glue
6. Scissors
7. Ink and brush
8. Watercolor
9. Construction paper

Have the students select and draw a number of the objects (three to six) in the room. Draw one object on each piece of the cut paper. Draw only the outline and surface details of the object. Don't add any value changes or shading to the drawings. The drawing can have only one bright color. Watercolor may be added to the white paper or the object may be drawn on brown or gray construction paper.

Leaving the outline on the rectangular piece of paper, cut the drawings in halves or thirds and stack the parts together. Each student then selects some real materials to add to the collage.

On the tag board draw a large oval around the outside edge, so the oval is 12" x 18" approximately. Ask the students to imagine a still life flattened to the table. By leaving the drawings on the paper with the corners they have in a sense flattened the bottle to the table since the corners of the paper will seem like a table top in the collage.

Reassemble the cut drawings with the real materials inside the oval, building a composition by placing one-half of the drawn object on the left side and the other half on the right side, or shift the drawn parts one inch to two inches so the lines no longer match up. The edges of the pieces may overlap the border of the oval, making a jagged edge.

When the parts are assembled, the blank white of the drawn objects may be changed to a wood grain texture by drawing on them, or a lace texture by shaping real fabric into the outline. Newspaper can be cut out to fit inside a shape or beside a shape. Ink or watercolor may also be used to alter the surface

The surface can be varnished to flatten it down and protect it with acrylic matte medium or matte varnish; they are virtually the same. The medium looks milky white but dries clear. Add a small amount of water to the medium (1/4 C. medium, 1 Tbs. water), and put a thin coat on with a soft, flat brush.

GOALS

The students must make informed decisions dependent on their previous knowledge from other lessons. In addition, they are making spontaneous choices about how things go together as they make the collage.

They are using both creative and critical thinking skills. In addition their technical knowledge of materials is improved and extended.

SUMMARY OF STEPS

1. Collect collage materials.
2. Draw single objects on pieces of paper.
3. Cut drawings in halves and thirds.
4. Draw an oval on the tag board.
5. Reassemble the drawings and collage materials on the oval.
6. Use colored paper for drawings or add watercolor.
7. Add texture to objects.
8. Use real fabrics in the collage.
9. Surface can be varnished.

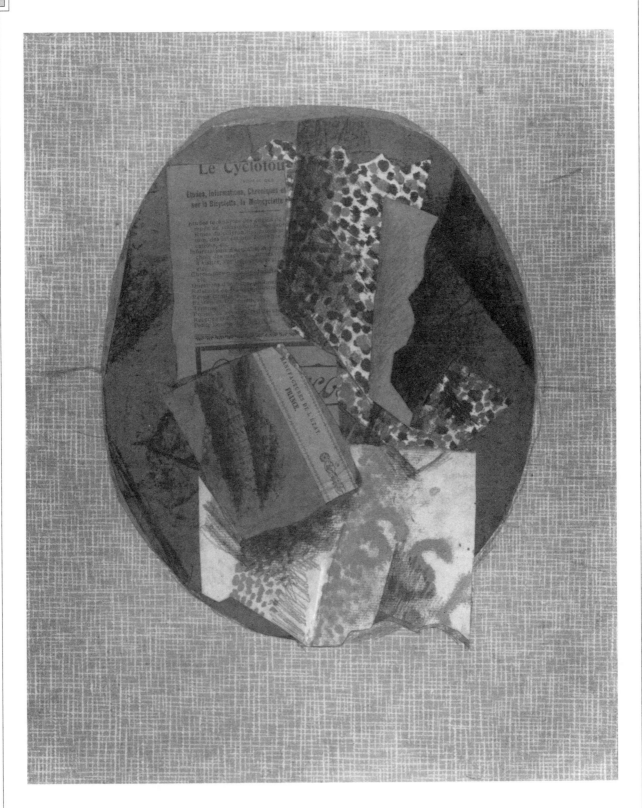

Georges Braque, French, 1882–1963, *Collage,* composed of charcoal, graphite, oil paint and watercolor on a variety of cut laid and wove paper elements laid down on dark tan board, c.1912, 35.1 x 27.9 cm. Gift of Mrs. Gilbert W. Chapman, 1947.879. Photograph © 1995, The Art Institute of Chicago. All rights reserved.

Henry Moore, *Woman in Shelter in Winter*, 1941, ink, watercolor, and crayon on paper, 7 1/4" x 6 3/4" (18.4 x 17.1 cm.). San Francisco Museum of Modern Art. Bequest of Elise S. Haas, 91.174.

BLIND WAX DRAWING

BRIEF OVERVIEW

This exercise can be frustrating before it is rewarding. It often surprises students when they discover recognizable images in their drawings. The more they do this exercise the better they will become at blindly drawing images. Their hand-and-eye coordination will improve markedly, and surprisingly enough, they will have more and more recognizable shapes in their drawings. The students should do the exercises Continuous Line Drawing and Scribbled Line Drawing before they do this one.

THE SETUP

Set up a large still life on a table in the middle of the room and circle the student's desks around it so everyone can see a section. Give each student a piece of wax and a piece of tag board. Ask them to stand up to draw and not rest their drawing arms on the table.

Before you start drawing, ask the students to think about what section they want to draw. Ask them to decide where to start, then which direction to move across the still life. Have them decide in advance how many objects they would like to draw. After they have looked at the subject for five minutes have them start.

They may look at the paper once, and that is to locate the wax on a starting point. After that they are to look only at the objects they are drawing, and not back at the paper. They are to move the wax on the paper as if they are drawing with a pencil. They must imagine what they are drawing in their heads because they aren't to look at the paper, and if they do look at the paper there won't be much to see since the wax is clear. Have them choose one object to draw at a time and rub the shape firmly into the paper.

Remind them to think about moving their hands slowly across the paper, up or down, left or right, to draw what they are seeing. Draw the object using lines that are crisscrossing the object's surface or circling it with ellipses. They are not to draw the outline of the object, rather they are to draw a solid form of each object.

SUPPLIES

1. 18" x 18" tag board
2. Small piece of wax (paraffin)
3. Ink and brush
4. Small jar or dish

When they feel that they have drawn as much as they can, they put a small amount of ink in a dish or jar, and using the brush, paint over the entire drawing.

There will probably be a lot of whining and complaining, but encourage them to keep at it and keep working. The results will surprise them.

University Student, Blind Wax Drawing

GOALS

Every student is equally successful and unsuccessful in this exercise. They see the drawing in their minds but the paper has a different image. This exercise is extremely good in building visual awareness and hand-eye coordination skills.

SUMMARY OF STEPS

1. Ask the students to look at the still life.
2. Plan what objects to draw.
3. They will draw with wax.
4. They may not look at their paper.
5. They should stand to draw.
6. They draw the objects as if they are solids.
7. For each object they crisscross the paper rubbing firmly with the wax to form it.
8. When they finish, they use the ink and the brush to cover the entire drawing.

RUBBINGS AND COLLAGE

BRIEF OVERVIEW

This exercise separates processes that can be used together or individually. Rubbings are transfers taken from real surfaces. The rubbing can be the end product or the rubbing can be used to texture a collage. In the Cubist Collage exercise, the rubbings could be used to texture the drawings. Rubbings allow you to make your own textures.

In this collage each form or object is cut-out and then reassembled. Each piece in the collage must be cut out of its previous background. It is then up to the students to reconstruct the pieces into a new composition whose order and arrangement they will make up.

THE SETUP

For rubbings, use rice paper or tracing paper. Thick papers are harder to get the texture or image to lift off the surface. Have the students select surfaces that seem textured, rough or uneven. Place the paper on the surface and hold it or tape it firmly in place. Gently rub the flat lead stick back and forth with enough pressure to pick up the texture but not so much that they rip the paper.

A field trip is a good time to accumulate textures. If the students have paper and pencils or the lead stick with them, they can get textures off walls, manhole covers, and other things on the street. A cemetery can be a popular place to do rubbings as the stones have carved designs on them that lift off nicely.

For the collage, have the students go through magazines and select images that they want in the collage. Cut the pages out and then cut the images out of the page background. A shoe box is a good place to store

SUPPLIES

1. Paper or tag board
2. Rice paper or tracing paper
3. Lead sticks or 6B pencils
4. Glue
5. Magazines
6. Scissors

Pencil Rubbing

the little cut-out pieces until they are ready to paste them together. The collage can be built on a rubbing, a piece of construction paper (white or colored) or a piece of tag board. Have the students assemble their cut out pieces.

If the collage is constructed on a piece of white drawing paper, the students may use their pastels to add color by rubbing pastel over and around the cut-out pieces. To add pastel, take a piece of scrap paper and wipe the pastel on it a few times back and forth. Use the stump or a tissue wrapped around a finger to pick up the pastel off the paper and then transfer the color on to the surface of the collage. This method puts color on very slowly and evenly. The students can mix colors together by overlapping layers of color. If they put yellow on for example and then rub red gently on top of it they will have an orange. The surface will have a softer glow by adding pastel in this way.

GOALS

This type of precision cutting improves hand-eye coordination. In addition the gluing is more difficult and demanding. The students must be patient and plan the collage, carefully balancing the pieces. They are using critical thinking and developing their decision making skills.

SUMMARY OF STEPS

1. Make rubbings with thin paper and lead sticks or pencils.
2. Select real surfaces with texture to rub.
3. For collage, cut out magazine photos.
4. Cut the individual image out of the background.
5. Reassemble the images
6. Rub in pastel for color.

WOVEN NEWSPAPER

BRIEF OVERVIEW

It is often difficult to find art projects that can combine with other parts of the curriculum and not compromise the art or the other subject. This one may solve that problem. First, it uses real material from the social and political world, the newspaper. Second, the students express their point of view by the subjects they choose to use. Third, they are making an art piece out of information about the world they live in. This collage puts two opposites together or two opposing views or two opposite life styles. It's a way to talk about difference and uniting difference.

THE SETUP

You may use newspaper or newspaper and magazines or only magazines. Each student should select a subject. You may want to give them a frame of reference to work within if you are tying this to Science, Geography, or History. Then with the subject and its opposite in mind they select pages or articles from the newspaper or the magazines to use in their woven collages. The sections should be chosen for meaning and content.

First decide on the outside dimensions of the weaving. The selected newspaper pages must be cut or ripped into strips. Each student decides what width to make the strips, 1/2", 3/4", 1", and so on. They will need continuous lengths to weave with. Glue the strips together, making lengths that will stretch across the weaving the length of the outside dimensions. They should make two piles of strips, one for the width and one for the length.

When they are choosing what to put together, they may want to consider any colors that are showing, the size of the type, and any other features of the pages that are visually attractive or interesting.

To start the weaving, tape or glue one set of the strips vertically, side by side, to the top edge of a piece of cardboard or heavy tag board. To leave a border, tape the strips two to three inches in from the top and leave the same border on either side and the

SUPPLIES

1. Newspaper
2. Glue
3. Tag board or card board
4. Scissors

bottom. To leave a border, this board should be two or three inches bigger on all sides than the finished weaving. Using the other pile of strips, weave them one at a time through the set glued on one end to the board. It is easiest to weave the strips through the open bottom of the hanging strips and then slide them up, snugging each strip next to the one above it. Secure the final strip with tape or glue so the weaving will hold to together and not slide apart.

If you use a black or colored ground on the board to start with, it sets off the weaving nicely when they are done and solves the framing and presentation problem. Construction paper can be glued over tag board and pressed in place with books while it dries to make a background.

GOALS

Students must exercise decision-making skills in the material and subject choices. They must research their ideas and plan their compositions.

SUMMARY OF STEPS

1. Select the focus of the weaving.
2. Select newspaper pages to use.
3. Make two piles of strips.
4. Decide on the dimensions of the weaving.
5. Make strips into lengths to weave.
6. Select back board and color of board.
7. Attach one set of strips to top of board.
8. Weave second set through first set.
9. Secure bottom or last strip woven in.

Laurie Anderson, American, born 1947, *New York Times, Horizontal/China Times, Vertical*, collage composed of cut, pasted and woven newspaper strips, 1971–1979, 76.2 x 55.9 cm. Margaret Fisher Endowment, 1992.745.

Material Option:

Rex Amos' collage on the facing page was composed by cutting each individual image completely out of its original background. The images were then reassembled in a new composition. The collage was glued together with a light layer of Elmers glue on rice paper and then sent through a printing press under some 300 pounds of pressure where a layer of transparent ink was printed on the entire surface of the collage. At the same time during this printing process the collage was glued to a large piece of Arches printing paper which created a large border around the image. When the ink dried the artist rubbed layers of pastel into the collage and the immediate border of the image.

The students may add color to their collages by rubbing a chalk pastel on a scrap piece of construction paper to transfer the color. Then to pick up the color they use the stump, a soft cloth or a tissue wrapped tightly around the end of their finger. Rub the stump or tissue into the color and then transfer the color on the stump to the collage. Rub gently and slowly. They will need to go back and forth between the area of pastel and their collage to wipe in enough pastel to get a rich color on the collage.

Rex Amos, American, b. 1935, *The Clowns of Dublin,* chiné colle, collage, and pastel, 1989. Image 13 1/2" w x 12 1/2" h, on Rives paper 22" x 30". Courtesy of the Artist and Magnolia Editions, Oakland, CA.

Portrait of Sandy Brooke, Jeffrey Clem, Grade 4, Pen & Ink

SECTION SIX:
Portrait/Pastel

*Sarah Freilich, Grade 3, Pastel Portrait After
Portrait of a Woman, The Green Stripe, Henri Matisse*

PLANES OF THE FACE

BRIEF OVERVIEW

The face and the head are very difficult to draw. The first problem arises because there aren't any lines on the face to follow. The second problem is the features of the face are on a curved rather than flat surface. A third level of difficulty presents itself as the students try to draw the eyes or nose without first defining all the parts.

Drawing the face is a volume problem. The head is not a circle or an oval but more of a sculptured ball. It's round, it has depth and the features of the face are not on straight horizontal or vertical lines as much as they are on lines more like the longitude and latitude lines on the earth.

If the students can at first translate the entire volume of the head to a flat piece of paper, they can later add the features and create a more realistic drawing. Julio Gonzalez's drawing, *Screaming Head* on the following page is a wonderful example of simplifying and separating geometrically the planes of the face. This cubist drawing is formed out of hard edges and definite planes folded where the shape of the head changes.

It is helpful to do the lessons on Crosshatching Practice, Chiaroscuro I and II, and Beginning Perspective prior to doing this one.

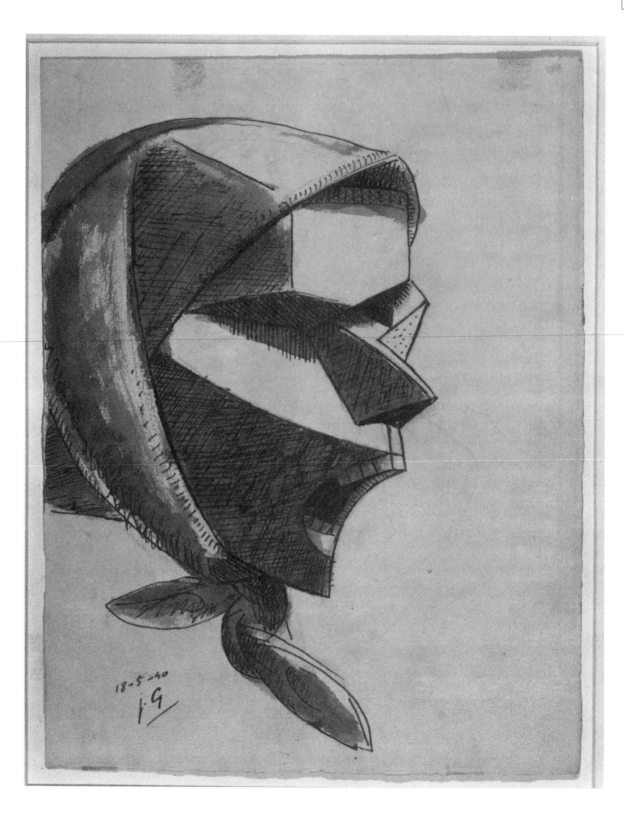

Julio Gonzalez, Spanish, 1876–1942, *Screaming Head,* pen and black ink, with brush and gray wash, over graphite, on off-white laid paper, 1940, 31.6 x 24 cm., McKee Fund, 1957.358. Photograph © 1995, The Art Institute of Chicago. All rights reserved.

THE SETUP

If you are comfortable with students' examining their faces, do the following exercise: Have the students place their hands on their foreheads. They are going to explore their head by noting what surfaces on the face push out and what areas are indented.

Imagine the head as a volleyball: The forehead is furthest out or a front plane. The eyebrows are on this top or front plane also, but the eyes are indented into the surface. The eye is drawn in three parts. There is the top eyelid and then the eye ball itself, followed by the lower eyelid and area under the eye.

The cheeks stand further out than the eyes. They start at the outside edge of the bottom of the eye. Another plane forms the side of the face. Have the students move their hands from the front cheek back along the side of the face. They should run into the middle of the ear. Have the students move their hand from the top of their eyebrows across the side of the heads, to the back of the head. They will run into the top of their ear.

The nose has three parts, the top and two sides. Have the students take their hands from the bridge of their nose, down the nose to the tip and then over to the right side, back up to the top and over to the left side of the nose. They can feel the three planes of the nose.

Move down the cheeks to under the nose where the lips are located. There are two lips, the top lip and the bottom lip. Move to the chin from the lips. Following the contours of the face in under the lips, out over the chin. Follow the chin line towards the back of the head. You will run into the bottom of the ears and you can feel the shape of the chin changing.

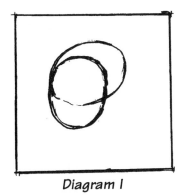
Diagram I

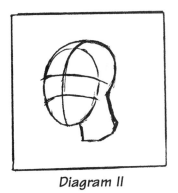
Diagram II

Diagram III

The diagrams will help you with the location of the facial features. The head is composed of two overlapping ovals. The eyes are placed halfway down the face. The nose is two-thirds of the way down from the top of the head. The lips fit under the nose. The tops of the ears are directly across from the tops of the eyes and the bottoms of the ears are across from the bottom of the nose.

Drawing Option I:

Have the students draw two overlapping ovals as in the diagram and ask them to try to fit the facial features on the heads. The more they practice placing the features on the face the easier this all become.

Drawing Option II:

Have the students copy Julio Gonzalez's drawing. If it helps, give each student a photocopy of the drawing to look at.

Drawing Option III:

Ask the students to map out the planes of their faces. Sometimes it is helpful to start with a drawing of a cube and form the head inside the cube.

Paul Cezanne was very interested in how the planes of the face turned in and out. His drawing is much softer and more realistic than Julio Gonzalez's but you can see where he divides the facial planes by using shading and crosshatching. The shading turns the form in and out. Julio Gonzalez does the same by separating the planes with more severe value changes.

Drawing Option IV:

Have the students copy the Cezanne portraits. Give them all photocopies to look at if possible.

GOALS

Students study the construction of the face in terms of planes. They practice drawing the face by copying the work of two famous artists. Artists for centuries learned their trade by making copies of the masters who went before them. Students in Europe before the turn of the century would spend hours in the Louvre copying the styles of Titian, Raphael, Delacroix, and Ingres.

SUMMARY OF STEPS

1. Discuss the planes of the face.
2. Students feel the planes on their faces.
3. Students draw a head like the diagrams.
4. Have students map out the planes of their faces in severe cubist separation.

Paul Cezanne, French, 1839–1906, *Sketchbook: Self-Portrait and Portrait of the Artist's Son, Chappuis 615,* pencil, stains, 1878–82, 12.4 x 21.7 cm. Arthur Heun Fund, 1951.1. Photograph © 1995, The Art Institute of Chicago. All rights reserved.

HAIR

Hair is a texture problem. You don't really draw hair, rather you invent it through a mark making process. Hair has depth that is hard to outline. The strand texture of hair can be created by overlapping lines of different widths and lengths. Stacking lines can also be effective. The lines can be wavy or straight.

The material you use to draw with will also influence the character of the line. Some artists invent and then construct their own tools to draw with. For instance, you can take denim fabric squares and roll them up allowing the frayed edge to remain at one end. This tool can be dipped in ink and loosely dragged in the direction you want the hair to be arranged. The loose quality of this kind of line looks more natural and not as stiff as a directly drawn line.

Instead of a pen you can use a stick dipped in ink and this tool will give you irregular marks and lines. A piece of fabric can be pounced on paper after either being dipped in ink or wiped through compressed charcoal. Vine charcoal can be wiped onto the area for the hair and then a rolled piece of fabric can be pounced into it to break the surface up and create an uneven texture.

The hair must curve over the shape of the head, and it is important to consider how far to draw the hair off the skull. Pierre Bonnard's drawing on the facing page is a good example of how to form hair with pen and ink.

SUMMARY OF STEPS

1. Copy Julio Gonzalez's drawing.
2. Start by mapping it out in pencil.
3. Use pen and ink to copy the qualities of the drawing.
4. Copy the Paul Cezanne drawing in pencil.
5. Use a hatching stroke to make the planes on the face.
6. Practice making hair by copying Bonnard.

Pierre Bonnard, French, 1867–1947, *Lady with Curly Hair,* brush and gray wash, on ivory wove paper, 22.4 x 19.5 cm. Bequest of Grant J. Pick, 1963.398. Photograph © 1995, The Art Institute of Chicago. All rights reserved.

USING VALUE TO SHAPE THE FACE

BRIEF OVERVIEW

This exercise will use the techniques studied in the Planes of the Face, Chiaroscuro and Reversed Charcoal exercises. Sometimes it is easier to draw form by subtracting instead of adding. Vine charcoal is best to use because it is easy to manipulate with erasing and then adding charcoal back into the drawing.

THE SETUP

The students start the way they did in the Chiaroscuro exercise, but this time they draw two overlapping circles and fill them in with vine charcoal. Rub the charcoal on gently, cross-hatching the strokes to cover the circle with a dark value of charcoal. Putting the charcoal on with too much pressure creates a lot of charcoal dust. There will be some dust, but it will be easier to control; it can be rubbed into the paper.

Using the kneaded eraser, find the center of the circle and draw a thin elliptical line across the ball. This line locates the eyes. Now the students can sculpt the eyes along that line by erasing the charcoal. Leave an area between the eyes for the bridge of the nose and erase the top plane of the nose. Add the eyebrows back in with the vine charcoal. Use the vine charcoal to draw the lines that shape the eye. To reduce the thickness of the line made by the charcoal, take the stump, and, using the tip, wipe off the excess charcoal—thus forming a fine line to shape the eye.

Use the dirty stump to build the side planes of the nose from the top plane down either side. The stump is nice to work with as it easier to control than the bulky charcoal and it makes a very soft gray. If you don't have the art kit, stumps can be made out of drawing paper and tissues. Roll up a small piece of drawing paper, cone shaped, and cover the pointed end with a tissue that has been folded over; tape the tissue to the rolled paper on the shaft. Make the tip tight so you can control it. Continue to lift charcoal out with the kneaded eraser and add it back in where needed.

SUPPLIES

1. 12" X 18" white paper
2. Vine charcoal
3. Kneaded erasers
4. 6B and 3B pencils
5. Plastic erasers
6. Chamois or tissues
7. Stump

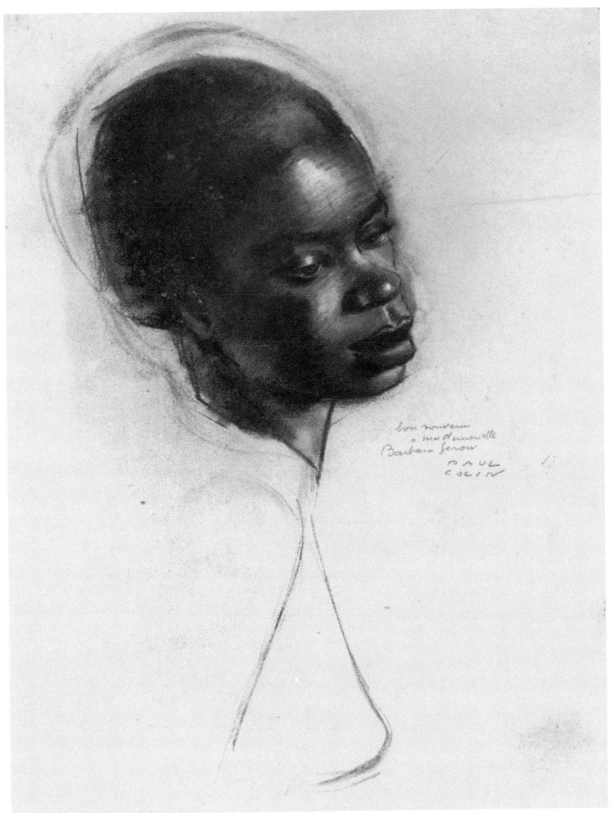

Figure of a Woman, ca. 1930 by Paul Colin, French, 1892–1985, black and white crayon on light beige paper. The Frederick and Lucy S. Herman Foundation. Muscarelle Museum of Art, College of William and Mary in Virginia.

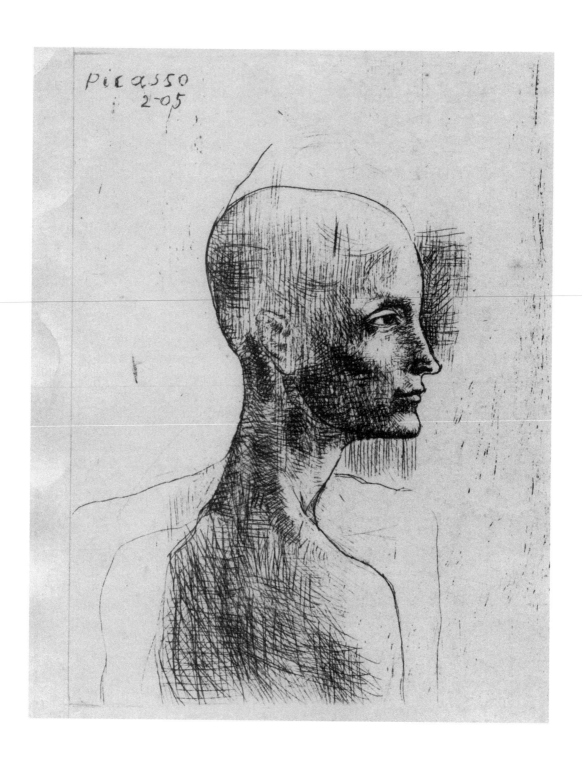

Pablo Picasso, Spanish, born 1881, *Bust of a Man*, etching, 5" x 6 1/2" Courtesy of the San Francisco Museum of Modern Art.

Use the kneaded eraser to pull out the charcoal where the top of the cheeks should be and then use the stump to gray the area on the sides of the cheeks. Erase out the tip of the nose and the lips. darken under the nose and under the bottom lip.

Start the neck at the bottom of the ears. Add a couple lines for the neck making one side light and one side dark.

As the students move around the ball, erasing and adding charcoal, have them try to form the space out of light and dark planes instead of lines. The top planes should be light and the back or receding planes should be darker. The face is not like the Grand Canyon. The distance between top and back plane may sometimes only be an eighth of an inch to half an inch. The face is constructed out of subtle changes. The charcoal moves in and out across the surface creating the planes of the face.

Roll the kneaded eraser across the top of the head to unevenly remove charcoal and to help in drawing the hair.

OPTION I

Cross-hatching is another way to create value on the planes of the face. In the exercises on Cross-hatching, the students learned how to build a surface up with overlapping layers of hatching marks.

To start, draw a circle with the 3B pencil. Apply one layer of strokes vertically and one layer of strokes horizontally across the circle. Use the tissue, the chamois, or your bare finger and gently rub across the marks, smearing the pencil.

Use the plastic eraser to remove the top and light planes of the face. Using the stump, rub the pencil marks to darken under the top planes for a shadow—places like under the eye socket, under the end of the nose, below the cheek, under the bottom lip. Darken the top lip, leaving the center of the bottom lip light. Then add a layer of strokes diagonally to the side planes of the face with the 6B pencil—first on either side of the forehead where the forehead changes from the front plane to the side plane, then on the plane between the top of the cheeks and the ears towards the back of the head. Darken under the chin on the neck, which pushes the chin more forward than the neck.

OPTION I: SUMMARY OF STEPS

1. Draw two overlapping circles.
2. Cross-hatch it once vertically and once horizontally.
3. Rub the pencil to smear it.
4. Use the plastic eraser and carve out the features.
5. Add 6B pencil to the side planes of the head to darken them.
6. Add the neck.

Max Beckmann, German, 1884–1950, *Self-portrait*, pen and black ink on cream laid paper, 1917, 38.7 x 31.6 cm. Gift of Mr. and Mrs. Allan Frumkin, 1975.1127. Photograph © 1995, The Art Institute of Chicago. All rights reserved.

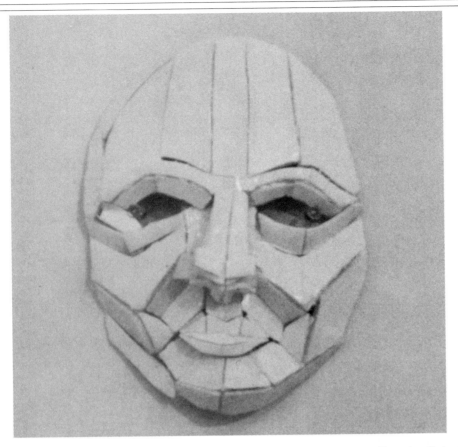

Brooke Cutsforth, University Student Drawing I, Model of Planes of the Face

GOALS

To understand how the planes of the face fit together. To accentuate the planes by using light and dark values. To model the face by erasing the features instead of drawing lines that will seem too harsh. This exercise improves creative thinking and visual memory.

SUMMARY OF STEPS

1. Draw two overlapping circles.
2. Fill them in with vine charcoal.
3. Find the center of the circle and draw the eyes there.
4. Erase the shapes of the features out of the charcoal.
5. Use the charcoal to add lines.
6. Use the stump to reduce thickness of lines.
7. Use the stump to darken under features.
8. A light plane needs a gray or dark plane next to it.
9. Imagine the way the surface of your face goes in and out.
10. Add the neck and shade one side.

PASTEL PORTRAITS

BRIEF OVERVIEW

If the students have done the exercises Planes of the Face and Using Value to Shape the Face, they will by now have a good sense of the proportions of the face. Using color to form the face, poses many of the same problems that occured in manipulating value to shape the face. There are light and dark colors, or light and dark values of one color. Color is lightened by adding white, and darkened by adding the complement or a darker value of the color (add dark green to light green). Black pastel tends to be greasy, and it is hard to use in mixing.

The students should choose different colors for the planes of the face. Use light colors for the top planes and medium to dark colors for the side planes. They may leave white areas between planes if they wish.

THE SETUP

For a subject, use photos out of a magazine or color copies of original portraits by Henri Matisse and Vincent van Gogh. Both these artists used color expressively, and often without any reference to true skin tones.

The students start with the HB pencil, drawing the outline of the face and noting the places where one plane turns into another. Draw a large head, neck, and shoulders. Have the drawing fill the paper. The pastels are bulky and are easier to use in larger spaces.

Start with a light pastel on a top plane followed by a medium to dark color on the sides of the plane or on the plane next to it. Apply the pastel in light overlapping strokes, making two or three layers. In pastel drawing the students build the surface up from light to dark. It is easy to cover and change a light color, but not so easy to cover or change a dark color. The kneaded eraser can be used to pull some of the color out, but a small shadow will remain from a dark color.

SUPPLIES

1. 12" x 18" pink or white construction paper
2. Pastels
3. Kneaded eraser
4. HB pencil
5. Hand rag
6. Tissues

Andrew Thomson, Grade 3, Pastel, Portrait
After a Drawing by Henri Matisse

After the students form the face with light, medium, and dark colors, have them select colors for the background. They can make one-half of the back ground light and one-half dark, or suggest choosing a complementary color for each side of the face (Red next to Green, Blue next to Orange, or Yellow next to Purple).

Use spray fix to set the chalk, or inexpensive hair spray to fix the drawing. If the students put the chalk on too lightly and in only one layer, the fix will melt some of the surface away. They should go over the areas in their drawings once or twice with the pastel. Encourage them to build up the surface in layers of pastel. Pastels are better layered gently and with light pressure than put on like crayons. Rubbing too hard with a chalk pastel will create a large amount of dust on the paper. No matter what you do there will be some chalk dust, but it is easier to deal with small amounts. A solution to the dust problem is while the students are drawing, rubbing the dust into the paper or gently shaking the dust into a garbage can.

To avoid dust, very lightly dampen the paper before starting the drawing and that will help control the dust. School paper is often thin so dampen lightly and a little at a time.

GOALS

The students will interpret the planes of the face into color by selecting light and dark colors to place side by side. They will improve their decision-making skills and their hand-eye coordination, and see the differences between color changes and black-and-white value changes to construct the facial planes.

SUMMARY OF STEPS

1. Select a portrait to draw.
2. Outline the face in pencil.
3. Map out the planes.
4. Choose light colors for top planes.
5. Choose medium or dark colors for back planes.
6. Dampen paper lightly to avoid dust.
7. Choose background colors.
8. Spray fix.

Caricatures of Bandits, by Marco Ricci (Italian, 1676–1729), pen and brown ink, wash. The Frederick and Lucy S. Herman Foundation, Muscarelle Museum of Art, College of William and Mary in Virginia.

CARICATURE

BRIEF OVERVIEW

Sometimes it is easier to draw the face by exaggerating the features; this is what caricature does. It shouldn't be used to make fun of others, although throughout history political cartoonists have attacked kings and others in positions of power with their caricatures. Caricature was used to point out inequities—not merely to make fun of another person.

Monet's *Caricature of a Man with a Large Nose* is part of a series of drawings he did very early in his career—and probably for money. Franz Kline, the famous abstract expressionist painter, also did caricatures, which were displayed in a restaurant in New York for years.

Leonardo da Vinci drew incredibly interesting portraits of people with very unusual features. You can probably find these drawings in the library. Marco Ricci, an Italian artist, was making caricatures between 1690 and 1729. Caricature is as old as painting and drawing, a delightful way to learn to draw the face.

Nick Stember, Grade 4, Thinking While Copying Leonardi da Vinci Caricatures.

Claude Monet, French, 1840–1926, *Caricature of a Man with a Large Nose*, graphite on tan wove paper, c. 1855/56, 24.9 x 15.2 cm. Gift of Carter H. Harrison, 1933.895. Photograph © 1995, The Art Institute of Chicago. All rights reserved.

THE SETUP

Using the examples by Monet and Marco Ricci, let the students copy the drawings. Make photocopies for them to use. If you can find other caricatures in the library, or if the students can find some, use them also.

Let the students pick the medium they want to draw with. After they practice the facial features, ask them to try one of their own, but tell them it has to be an imaginary person or a political figure. They can't select a fellow student.

Have the students bring in pictures from the newspaper of senators and congress people, even the President. Then they can draw directly on the newspaper photo with pencil which they later can look at and translate onto another piece of paper.

Myngoc Le, Grade 4 Drawing Marilyn Monroe

Copying is actually a traditional way that drawing was taught. Artists were sent to the museums to learn by copying old masters. The experience of making a drawing, instructs the students' memory and furthers their understanding of how to draw. The act of drawing improves the hand-eye coordination which in return improve drawing skills.

GOALS

To improve the students' understanding of facial features. To improve their hand-eye coordination.

Travis Drawing a Portrait from a Copy,
Grade 5

SUMMARY OF STEPS

1. Talk to students about caricature.
2. Have them look in the library for examples.
3. Ask the students to bring in newspaper photos of political figures.
4. Make copies of the examples in the book.
5. Have the students copy the examples.
6. Let them pick what medium to use.
7. The students can draw directly on the newspaper photos, changing the features.
8. They then redraw the political caricature by looking at their own changes.

Max Beckmann, German, 1884–1950, *The Bathers*, black and white chalk on blue wove paper, 1928, 87 x 58 cm. Gift of Mr. and Mrs. Stanley Freehling, 1964.202. Photograph © 1995, The Art Institute of Chicago. All rights reserved.

PASTEL HOUSES

BRIEF OVERVIEW

Before doing this exercise have the students do the exercises on Two-point Perspective, Houses and Buildings, and Cross-hatching.

This exercise could be tied to other parts of the curriculum, for example if they are studying a country that doesn't use the Western-style house you could use those house as subjects for the drawing. Beverly Buchanan's houses were shacks that people built by hand. These shacks were kept up by the people who lived in them and were not called shacks because they were run down or dirty, but because they were constructed from scrap lumber and found objects. Being made by hand without the use of many tools, they have a very unfinished, unconventional look to them. When added to the independent spirit of the people who make them, the unconventional look lends them a certain charm and strength of human spirit.

THE SETUP

Using the 3B pencil, have the students draw a large house or two houses. Use the pastels to color the house. Each side to the house should be a different color. The windows may be dark or light.

Colors of pastel may be overlapped, for example, yellow over red will change it to an orange. Hot pink and turquoise will make purple when mixed. To start pick colors to use as foundation colors and rub them into each area one at a time. The next layer of color may also be rubbed into the foundation but do so gently. A third layer should not be rubbed in but

SUPPLIES

1. White paper
2. 3B pencil
3. Pastels
4. Tissues
5. Hand rag

Beverly Buchanan, American 20th century painter, *Waterfront Shacks*, 1993, oil pastel on paper, 60" x 60", Courtesy of Steinbaum Krauss Gallery, New York.

laid down and left alone. At a certain point, rubbing dulls or muddies the color while just pulling the the chalk gently across the surface increases the intensity of the color.

SUMMARY OF STEPS

1. Select a dwelling.
2. Draw a large house or two.
3. Use different colors of pastel to separate the sides of the house.
4. Use pastel cross-hatched strokes to create grass.
5. Layer strokes for the sky and do not rub together.
6. Use black last to texture and outline.

Avoid rubbing pastels together to blend them if they begin to get muddy or dull. As a last step put a light layer on top of all of the mixtures to bring back the richer color. Don't rub the last layer of pastel, just wipe it on and leave it. Any light color can be wiped on a dark base. The base can be seen through this last layer, making the drawing richer looking. The students may prefer working in layers of marks and strokes like Beverly Buchanan. In that case don't rub the layers, just stack the strokes in layers.

For the grass and the sky don't rub the colors together at all. Put them on in overlapping or side-by-side strokes. Build the surface by adding color but not rubbing it into the paper.

Use black at the very end to outline areas or texture surfaces. Black gets very messy when rubbed, so it's best to use it at the end when there's less chance of its getting smeared.

GOALS

To study the diversity in people's homes. To use the pastel to separate the surfaces. To develop texture, using overlapping strokes of color. To practice two-point perspective. To challenge the students' decision-making skills.

Blake Shaw-Phillips, One-point Perspective, Grade 5

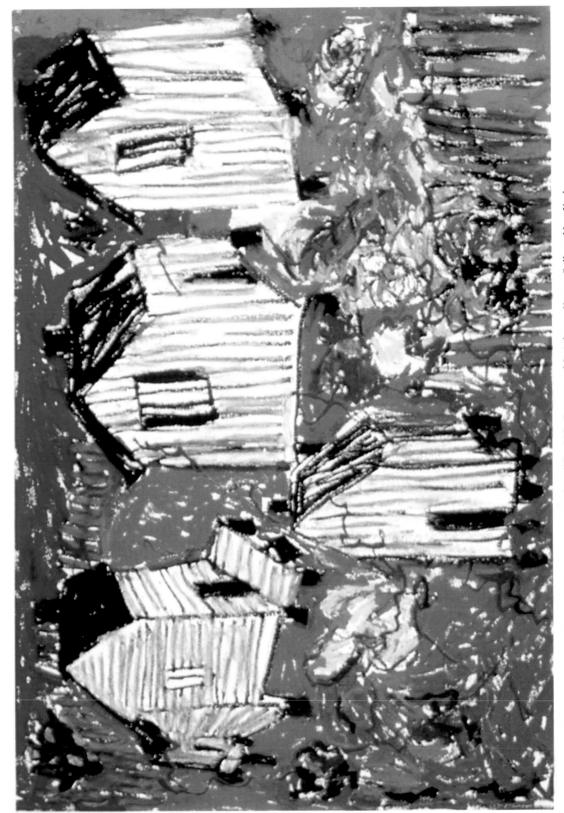

Beverly Buchanan, *Blue Lightning*, 1995, pastel on paper 25 1/2" x 38". Courtesy of Steinbaum Krauss Gallery, New York.

PASTEL STILL LIFE

BRIEF OVERVIEW

Use fruit and bowls for the still life, on a table cloth with something sitting behind it. Using round forms helps in arranging the students around the table, it gives everyone a good angle and view. Have the table below the student's eye level a little allowing them to see things more clearly.

Doing the exercises, Overlapping Shapes and Simple Still Life: Charcoal will prepare the students to do this exercise.

THE SETUP

Using a light pastel, the students make a full-size drawing of the fruit and bowl, filling their paper. Three or four students can share a box of 24 pastels easily. Pastels usually come in sticks that are 2 1/2 inches long. They should be broken in half for easier use.

In this drawing the pastels must be layered. There are many ways to layer pastels:

1. For an orange fruit. Without rubbing the pastel into the paper, cover the entire circle in light yellow. Then add a layer of light orange to the top and middle. Use a darker orange on the bottom and the middle. Use white on the top for a highlight.

2. Another way is to rub the first color into the paper with a tissue or finger, and then build on the first layer without rubbing the following colors.

3. The first three or four layers of pastel may be rubbed into the paper. Apply the last layer without rubbing it in; this makes the surface richer.

4. If an area on an orange is very dark, use a light layer of a dark color like green or blue rubbing it in and then cover it with red or orange as a top layer. The surface will look dark orange. If you rub the top layer of orange in, it will muddy and you will need to put another untouched layer of orange pastel on to get the surface to look orange.

5. Beware of rubbing opposite colors together (red and green, yellow and purple, blue and orange). They muddy the fastest. Any color may be put on any other color as long as you don't

SUPPLIES

1. Colored construction paper
2. Pastels
3. Tissues
4. Wet rag

277

rub them together. Rub them together if you want a muddy color for a base color or a shadow.

Have the students use the layering process to build the pastel up on every form in the drawing. Add color to the background and the foreground or table top. Opposite colors are often used as shadows. Placing opposites side by side electrifies the drawing. (Van Gogh was fond of purple shadows on yellow grass.)

Ask the students to try to get a range from light to dark on the fruit and bowl. The pastel may be applied off the corner of the chalk, at the square end or off the large side. When you are mixing colors, the chalks will get dirty. Use a tissue to wipe the colors off so the mixed mud on the chalk does not transfer onto the drawing.

By working light to dark, a light color placed on the drawing that is unwanted can be rubbed into the paper and covered with another color. It is harder to get rid of dark colors and pastels don't erase completely. To clean up areas of the drawing use the chamois to lift some of it out, or a tissue. We mainly cover up mistakes with new colors.

Pastels may be layered wet or dry; you can start by taking a damp sponge and lightly dampening the paper and then gently wipe the pastels on, or the students may place the first color on dry paper and then take a wet cloth wrapped around a finger and wash over the color. They must then let the area dry. They can add another layer of color on top of the dried area.

GOALS

To practice layering pastels and building up the surface of the still life with light and dark values. To develop patience in building a surface. New skills in manipulating color and space are developed by this exercise.

SUMMARY OF STEPS

1. Outline a still life in light pastel.
2. Use the layering process.
3. Use wet and dry layers.
4. Layer each form in a range of light to dark values.
5. Select color for background.
6. Opposite colors work well as shadows.
7. Carefully spray fix the drawing.

Simon Dinnerstein, *Red Pears*, 1987, conté crayon, colored pencil, pastel, crayola, oil pastel, 5 1/2″ x 6 3/8″. Collection of Lawrence and Ellen Benz, Bronxville, New York.

SECTION SEVEN:
Appendixes

Appendix I: Materials

Appendix II: Setting Up a Still Life

Appendix III: Glossary

George Wesley Bellows, American 1882–1925, *Elsie Speicher, Emma Bellows, and Marjorie Henri*, black crayon over touches of graphite, on cream wove paper, 1921, 44.1 x 52.6 cm. Gift of Friends of American Art Collection, 1922.5553. Courtesy of The Art Institute of Chicago.

APPENDIX I: MATERIALS

PAPER

Paper can be very expensive, and considering how much paper you will need to do these exercises, finding less expensive paper is important. The exercises in the book emphasize process more than product, so expensive paper is not really necessary or recommended. If you would like the students to experience the quality of better paper, you might want to treat yourself to finer paper for perhaps a single exercise. Meanwhile, white sulfite drawing paper of 60 lbs to 80 lbs. will work for most of the lessons on paper.

Use 150-lb tag board for ink, wet work, and gluing. Bristol board is the higher quality equivalent to tag board; it has a stiff, slick surface that is wonderful for ink or for rubbing pencil.

A substitute for charcoal paper, which can be expensive, is construction paper. Construction paper works well with pastels and charcoal. The students can choose between white or colors. Pink, purple, and black work well for portraits. Working wet on construction paper is not recommended; it tends to shred.

Rice paper is not very expensive and is excellent for making rubbings. Your school may have tracing paper on hand, which will also work. Any thin paper will transfer a texture. Construction paper is too thick but 60 lb drawing paper will often work. Bugra paper, from Rochester Art Supply, works well if your budget can afford it.

When shopping for papers, examine them for their color, rough or smooth surface, texture, and thickness. The best papers are made of a high rag content. They are also the most expensive.

THE ART KIT

Buying art supplies is often confusing and difficult for the beginner. In an effort to help teachers with this, we have put an art kit together that has all the drawing supplies except paper suggested for use in these exercises. Each student receives an individual kit. These kits can then be refilled by purchasing bulk orders of charcoal, pencils, erasers, and so on. The order form for the kit can be found at the end of the materials section.

CHARCOAL

Charcoal is available in three forms—vine, compressed, and charcoal pencils. Ritmo makes an excellent charcoal pencil. They are expensive, so they were not recommended for the exercises in this book.

Vine charcoal is made from hardwood. Bob's Fine Vine in the art kit is manufactured in a cottage industry by a young man now 16 years old in Eugene, Oregon. It is excellent charcoal. Occasionally part of the wood doesn't burn out completely and there may be a spot that is unusable on the stick. Those areas should be broken off. Vine is the least permanent of the three forms. It is excellent for organizing and mapping out a drawing. Its most redeeming feature is that it is highly correctable, and can be easily wiped off with a chamois or a tissue. Vine can, however, be pressed hard enough into school paper that a light shadow remains after erasing.

Compressed charcoal comes in stick form. The block style of the stick allows the artist to draw with the end, the long side, or the corner between two sides. It is darker and richer than vine. In addition, it is very difficult to remove. There will always be a shadow left after erasing.

Charcoal pencil is a wooden pencil with a charcoal point. It can be sharpened and makes a fine, dark line. The best charcoal leads are HB, B, or 3B sizes. When this lead gets to 6B, it is so soft it often breaks in the pencil shaft.

PENCILS AND GRAPHITE STICKS

Pencils and graphite sticks come in different degrees of hardness and softness; the H pencils are hard and the B pencils are soft. The soft B pencils start at HB, B, 2B, 3B, and so on to 9B. The 6B is about as soft as students can handle. The H leads get harder from H to 2H to 6H, where the line is very light and very thin. Draftspeople and architects tend to use the H leads, while artists prefer the B leads.

Graphite sticks are best in soft leads of B to 3B. They work very well for laying in large areas of value. They are also easier to use for rubbings than pencils. Pencil and graphite marks can be smudged, smeared, and erased.

ERASERS

An eraser is a drawing tool. Most exercises in this book discourage the teacher from giving students an eraser to remove marks until the end of the drawing.

THE KNEADED ERASER

The kneaded eraser absorbs charcoal when you press the eraser into the area to be removed and rub the area gently. Once the eraser is dirty, clean it by stretching it or pulling it like a piece of taffy, and then folding it back into a ball. It is better not to pull the eraser completely apart; it should be stretched just enough to perform its self-cleaning function. Being extremely pliable, this eraser can be formed into a point or other shapes, and used to draw with.

THE PLASTIC ERASER

This eraser will lift charcoal out when you rub over it. When the plastic eraser gets dirty, it stops erasing and begins smearing the charcoal or pencil. Simply rub the dirty area off the eraser on a clean piece of scratch paper until it is clean, and then continue to remove pencil or charcoal off the paper.

CHAMOIS

A chamois skin is not technically an eraser, although it can be used to remove vine charcoal and pastel. It will also lighten the value of charcoal when it is rubbed into charcoal. A chamois is made of leather and can be cleaned with warm, soapy water.

PENS AND INKS

Sumi ink is the recommended permanent ink for the exercises in this book. It is somewhat cheaper than India ink, and works the same for washes and line drawing.

Pen points come in a wide range of sizes and shapes. It is fun to experiment with different speedball points to see what kind of line they will make. The one in the kit is particularly good for fine line drawing.

SPRAY FIXATIVE

Workable fix helps to prevent smearing and keeps the powdery media like pastels and charcoal from dusting off. "Workable" means you can work back into the drawing after spray fixing it. Some areas cannot be erased out entirely, but other areas can be darkened and changed. This fix doesn't have a hard surface. Blair makes a no-odor spray fix that is less toxic to work with than some others. Another option is hair spray—the cheaper the better. The cheap hair sprays tend to have more lacquer in them, which is what you want to hold the pencil or charcoal to the surface. Hair spray is not a workable fixative.

CHALK PASTELS

Weber-Costello makes a box of 24 chalk pastels for about $8.00. They are perfectly fine for students. The pastel sticks should be broken in half before the students use them. The pastel is easiest to use when it fits between the thumb, forefinger, and middle finger. They dissolve in water and can be used wet or dry. They can be mixed by overlapping colored layers or they can be applied to scrap paper and transferred to the drawing with the stump.

SOLD TO:

Name _____

Street Address _____ **Apt/Suite** _____

City _____ **State/Province** _____ **Zip/Postal Code** _____

County _____ **Day Phone** _____

SHIP TO: Note-UPS will not deliver to a P.O. Box

Name _____

Street Address _____ **Apt/Suite** _____

City _____ **State/Province** _____ **Zip/Postal Code** _____

County _____ **Day Phone** _____

Special Instructions _____

Rochester Art Supply

rochester, n.y. 14614

Send Orders To:

Sandy Brooke
(agent for Rochester Art Supply)
2645 NW Ginseng Place
Corvallis, OR   97330

Payments:

We accept Visa, MasterCard and Discover Cards. In addition, we will accept Money Orders, Cashier's Checks and School District Checks. However, we <u>do not</u> accept personal checks or COD orders.

QTY.	DESCRIPTION	Unit Price	Amount
1 ea	Black Sumi Ink 2 oz	$4.50	
1 ea	Plastic Mixing Cup	.49	
1 ea	Large Kneaded Eraser	.65	
1 ea	White Plastic Eraser	.80	
1 ea	Chamois	.50	
1 ea	Pencil Sharpener	1.40	
1 ea	Conte French Stump	1.45	
1 ea	Speedball Penholder & Nib	2.60	
3 ea	Assorted Graphite Pencils	2.10	
1 ea	4B Graphite Sticks	.60	
1 ea	Compressed Charcoal	.58	
1 ea	Large Stick Bob's Fine Vine Charcoal	.75	
4 ea	Small Sticks Bob's Fine Vine Charcoal	1.00	
	Kit Retail Value		**$17.42**

* If ordering more than one kit, call for actual shipping charges.

Method of Payment

☐ Cashier's check or money order
☐ Visa
☐ Mastercard
☐ Discover Card

Credit Card#_____._____._____._____

Exp. Date_____ Phone # ( )_____

Signature_____

SPECIAL KIT PRICE	15.00
Shipping & Handling	* 4.75
Shipments within NYS include your sales tax rate or forward your exemption certificate.	
TOTAL	

APPENDIX II: SETTING UP A STILL LIFE

SELECTING OBJECTS

Objects that are good to use for beginning still life setups are oranges, grapefruits, bottles (wine bottles without labels), milk bottles, large and small vases, eggplants, cookie jars, onions, bowls, and basically round things without handles.

Students who have done the Cylinder exercises, including the Handles and Spouts section will be ready to draw pitchers, cups, sugar bowls, and objects with protruding parts.

Avoid boxes, toy trucks, and geometric shapes until the students have studied one- and two-point perspective.

ARRANGING THE ROOM

Option #1 for arranging the room

Place a medium-sized round table in the middle of a circle of student desks, with the objects placed in groupings of four and five on the table so that each student has a clear view of one section of the still life. Avoid placing objects with handles directly in front of the students. Try to give your students a side view of handles to start out with.

Option #2

Place four to five student desks in a semicircle around a small desk-size table with a still life of different sizes of objects. Try to keep their sitting position approximately four feet from the setup. By sitting at this distance, the students have a better view of the objects, making it easier for them to fill the page. This arrangement is good when students need to consider the spatial relationships of objects, their placement, and their proportions to other objects.

If seeing the shadows or the direction in which the light is falling is important, set up a still life of bottles painted white, black, and gray on a table with a white cloth or paper underneath. Use short and tall bottles, and try to have the students four to five feet away from at least three bottles. Painting the bottles white, black, or gray is helpful if the students need to define the surface with value changes. Glass is so reflective, it interferes and confuses beginning students about where to make the breaks in value from light to dark across the surface. The students can see more detail if they are in small groups around a small table.

If the room is small: Set up one long table in the middle of the room with all the students' desks lined up on either side and at the ends. Group the bottles in sections of four or five down the table. The students then concentrate on the bottles closest to their sitting positions. You will probably need a minimum of 12 to 18 bottles. Exercises Cross-hatching a Still Life, Ink Line Drawing, and Continuous Line Drawing can use this arrangement.

For value studies like Chiaroscuro, and Charcoal Still Life, the still life should be four objects sitting on a piece of fabric with one side to the light. The side of the objects closest to the light that is coming through the windows will therefore be the light side and have the hot spot, or place where the light strikes the form first, so that the other side is automatically designated the dark side.

For Wet Charcoal and Reversed Charcoal

Set up a still life with a white cloth or white piece of paper underneath it and a patterned cloth behind it. Use dark objects like black bottles, an eggplant, dark vases of blue or purple, or a Danish squash.

Sample Still Life Setup

Jerry Burris, Grade 4, Ink and Wax Still Life

Andrew Swanson, Grade 4,
Erased Pencil Still Life

APPENDIX III: GLOSSARY

abstract   In art, the rendering of images and objects in a stylized or simplified way, so that though they remain recognizable, their *formal* or *expressive* aspects are emphasized. Compare both *representational* and *nonobjective*.

Abstract Expressionism   A painting style of the late 1940s and early 1950s, predominantly American, characterized by its rendering of *expressive content* by *abstract* or *nonobjective* means.

acrylic   A plastic resin that, when mixed with water and pigment, forms an inorganic and quick-drying paint *medium*.

actual texture   As opposed to *implied* or *visual texture*, the literal tactile quality or feel of a surface, including the mark made by a drawing tool, and the addition of other materials such as sand or fabrics.

additive   1) In color, the adjective used to describe the fact that, when different *hues* of colored light are combined, the resulting mixture is higher in *key* than the original hues and brighter as well, and as more and more hues are added, the resulting mixture is closer and closer to white; 2) In sculpture, an adjective used to describe the process in which form is built up, shaped, and enlarged by the addition of materials, as distinguished from *subtractive* sculptural processes, such as carving.

aesthetic   Pertaining to the appreciation of the beautiful, as opposed to the functional or utilitarian, and, by extension, to the appreciation of any form of art, whether overtly "beautiful" or not.

arbitrary color   Color that has no *realistic* or natural relation to the object that is depicted, as in a blue horse or a purple cow, but which may have emotional or *expressive* significance.

arbitrary value   *Value* used on an object based on an intuitive response or compositional demand but not as a rendering of light on form.

arch   A curved, often semicircular architectural form that spans an opening or space built of wedge-shaped blocks, called *voussoirs*, with a *keystone* centered at its top.

Art Deco   A popular art and design style of the 1920s and 1930s associated with the 1925 Exposition Internationale des Arts Décoratifs et Industriels Modernes in Paris and characterized by its integration of organic and geometric forms.

Art Nouveau   The art and design style characterized by undulating, curvilinear, and organic forms that dominated popular culture at the turn of the century, and that achieved particular success at the 1900 International Exposition in Paris.

assemblage　An *additive* sculptural process in which various and diverse elements and objects are combined.

asymmetric balance　Balance achieved in a composition when neither side reflects or mirrors the other.

atmospheric perspective　A technique, often employed in landscape painting, designed to suggest *three-dimensional space* in the *two-dimensional space* of the *picture plane*, and in which forms and objects distant from the viewer become less distinct, often bluer or cooler in color, and contrast among the various distant elements is greatly reduced.

avant-garde　Those whose works can be characterized as unorthodox and experimental.

Baroque　A dominant style of art in Europe in the seventeenth century characterized by its theatrical, or dramatic, use of light and color, by its ornate forms, and by its disregard for *classical* principles of composition.

barrel vault　A masonry roof, constructed on the principle of the arch, that is, in essence, a continuous series of arches, one behind the other.

base line　An imaginary line on which a group of objects on one objects sits.

bas-relief　See *low relief*.

Bauhaus　A German school of design, founded by Walter Gropius in 1919 and closed by Hitler in 1933.

blind contour　A contour drawing where the artist never looks down at the paper but keeps their eye on the subject.

calligraphy　The art of fine handwriting.

Carolingian art　European art from the mid-eighth to the early tenth century, given impetus and encouragement by Charlemagne's desire to restore the civilization of Rome.

cartoon　As distinct from common usage—where it refers to a drawing with humorous content—any full-size drawing, subsequently transferred to the working surface, from which a painting or tapestry is made.

chiaroscuro　In drawing and painting, the use of light and dark to create the effect of three-dimensional, *modeled* surfaces.

classical line　A kind of line that is mathematical, precise, and rationally organized, epitomized by the vertical and horizontal grid, as opposed to *expressive line*.

Classical style In Greek art, the style of the fifth century B.C., characterized by its emphasis on balance, proportion, and harmony; by extension, any style that is based on logical, rational principles.

collage A work made by pasting various scraps or pieces of material—cloth, paper, photographs—onto the surface of the *composition*.

column A vertical architectural support, usually topped by a *capital*.

comparative process The basic critical tool of art history and criticism, in which works of art are compared and contrasted with one another in order to establish both continuities and similarities between various works or styles and significant differences or stylistic changes that have occurred historically.

composition The organization of the formal elements in a work of art.

conceptual art An art form in which the idea behind the work and the process of its making are more important than the final product.

Constructivism A Russian art movement, fully established by 1921, that was dedicated to *nonobjective* means of communication.

Conté crayon A soft drawing tool made by adding clay to graphite.

content The *subject matter* of a work of art. It may be symbolic, thematic having narrative, emotional or intellectual connotations but together they give the work its total meaning.

contour The visible border of an object in space.

cool colors Those colors in which blue is dominant, including greens and violets.

cross-contour line Line that defines the volumetric aspects of an object by running horizontal rather than vertical on the contours of the object.

cross-hatching Two or more sets of roughly parallel and overlapping lines, set at an angle to one another, in order to create a sense of three-dimensional, *modeled* space. See also *hatching*.

Cubism A style of art pioneered by Pablo Picasso and Georges Braque in the first decade of the twentieth century, noted for the geometry of its forms, its fragmentation of the object, and its increasing abstraction.

Dada An art movement that originated during World War I in a number of world capitals, including New York, Paris, Berlin, and Zurich, and that was so antagonistic to traditional styles and materials of art that it was considered by many to be "anti-art."

delineation The descriptive representation of an object by means of *outline* or *contour* drawing.

De Stijl   A Dutch art movement of the early twentieth century that emphasized abstraction and simplicity, reducing form to the rectangle and color to the *primaries*—red, blue, and yellow.

dome   A roof generally in the shape of a hemisphere or half-globe.

drypoint   An *intaglio* printmaking process in which the copper or zinc *plate* is incised by a needle pulled back across the surface, leaving a *burr*. The resulting *print* is also called a drypoint.

edition   In printmaking, the number of images authorized by the artist made from a single *plate*.

elevation   The side of a building, or a drawing of the side of a building.

encaustic   A method of painting with molten beeswax fused to the support after application by means of heat.

engraving   An *intaglio* printmaking process in which a sharp tool called a *burin* is used to incise the *plate*. The resulting *print* is also called an engraving.

environment   A form of art that is large enough for the viewer to move around in.

etching   An *intaglio* printmaking process in which a metal *plate* coated with wax is drawn upon with a sharp tool down to the plate and then placed in an acid bath. The acid eats away at the plate where the lines have been drawn, the wax is removed, and then the plate is inked and printed. The resulting *print* is also called an etching.

Expressionism   An art that stresses the psychological and emotional content of the work, associated particularly with German art in the early twentieth century. See also *Abstract Expressionism*.

expressive line   A kind of line that seems to spring directly from the artist's emotions or feelings—loose, gestural, and energetic—epitomized by curvilinear forms.

eye level   An imaginary horizontal line parallel to the student's eyes. Important to establish in drawing one- and two-point perspectives in a classroom.

Fauvism   An art movement of the early twentieth century characterized by its use of bold *arbitrary color*. Its name derives from the French word "fauve," meaning "wild beast."

figure-ground relationship   In a two-dimensional work, the relationship between a form or figure and its background.

fixative A thin liquid film sprayed over *pastel* and charcoal drawings to protect them from smudging.

fluting The shallow vertical grooves or channels on a *column*.

foreshortening The use of *perspective* to represent the apparent visual contraction of an object or figure that extends backward from the *picture plane* at an angle approaching the perpendicular.

form (1) The literal shape and mass of an object or figure. (2) More generally, the materials used to make a work of art, the ways in which these materials are utilized in terms of the formal elements (line, light, color, etc.), and the *composition* that results.

fresco Painting on plaster, either dry (*fresco secco*) or wet (*buon* or *true fresco*). In the former, the paint is an independent layer, separate from the plaster proper; in the latter, the paint is chemically bound to the plaster, and is integral to the wall or support.

frottage The process of making rubbings with graphite or crayon on paper from a textured surface. To transfer a real texture.

Futurism An early twentieth century art movement, characterized by its desire to celebrate the movement and speed of modern, industrial life.

gouache A painting medium similar to *watercolor*, but opaque instead of transparent.

Happening A spontaneous, often multimedia event, conceived by artists and performed not only by the artists themselves but often by the public present at the event as well.

hatching An area of closely spaced parallel lines, employed in drawing and *engraving*, to create the effect of shading or *modeling*. See also *cross-hatching*.

heightening The addition of *highlights* to a drawing by the application of white or a pale color.

Hellenistic art The art of the third and second centuries B.C. in Greece, characterized by its physical realism and emotional drama.

high contrast Maximum contrast between light and dark.

highlight The spot or one of the spots of highest *key* or *value* in a picture.

high relief In sculpture, where the figures and objects remain attached to a background plane and project off of it by at least half their normal depth.

hue A color, usually one of the six basic colors of the *spectrum*—the three *primary colors* of red, yellow, and blue, and the three *secondary colors* of green, orange, and violet.

idealism As opposed to *realism*, the representation of things according to a preconceived ideal form or type.

impasto Pigment applied very thickly to canvas or support.

implied line As opposed to *actual line*, a line created by movement or direction, such as the line established by a pointing finger, the direction of a glance, or a body moving through space.

impression In printmaking, a single example of an *edition*.

Impressionism A late nineteenth century art movement, centered in France, and characterized by its use of discontinuous strokes of color meant to reproduce the effects of light.

intaglio Any form of printmaking in which the line is incised into the surface of the printing plate, including *aquatint*, *drypoint*, *etching*, *engraving*, and *mezzotint*.

intensity The relative purity of a color's *hue*, and a function of a its relative brightness or dullness; also known as *saturation*.

intention What the artist means to convey in a work of art, as opposed, for instance, to the way the work is interpreted.

intermediate colors The range of colors on the *color wheel* between each *primary color* and its neighboring *secondary colors*; yellow-green, for example.

ka In ancient Egypt, the immortal substance of the human, in some ways equivalent to the Western soul.

key The relative lightness or darkness of a picture or the colors employed in it.

kinetic art Art that moves.

kitsch Sentimental, slick, and mass-produced art designed to appeal to the widest possible popular audience.

linear perspective A system for depicting *three-dimensional space* on a *two-dimensional* surface that depends upon two related principles: that things perceived as far away are smaller than things nearer the viewer, and that parallel lines receding into the distance converge at a *vanishing point* on the horizon line.

linocut A form of *relief* printmaking, similar to a *woodcut*, in which a block of linoleum is carved so as to leave the image to be printed raised above the surface of the block. The resulting *print* is also known as a *linocut*.

lithograph Any print resulting from the process of *lithography*.

lithography A printmaking process in which a polished stone, often limestone, is drawn upon with a greasy material; the surface is moistened and then inked; the ink adheres only to the greasy lines of the drawing; and the design is transferred to dampened paper, usually in a printing press.

local color As opposed to *optical* or *perceptual color,* the actual *hue* of an object, independent of the ways in which different conditions of light and atmosphere might affect it.

low contrast A minimum of contrast between light and dark, so that the image is either predominantly dark or predominantly light.

low relief In sculpture, where the figures and objects remain attached to a background plane and project off it by less than one-half their normal depth. See also *bas-relief.*

Mannerism The style of art prevalent especially in Italy from about 1525 until the early years of the seventeenth century, characterized by its dramatic use of light, exaggerated *perspective*, distorted forms, and vivid colors.

medium (1) Any material used to create a work of art. (2) In painting, a liquid added to the paint that makes it easier to manipulate.

metalpoint A drawing technique, also known as *silverpoint*, popular in the fifteenth and sixteenth centuries, in which a stylus with a point of gold, silver, or some other metal was applied to a sheet of paper treated with a mixture of powdered bones (or lead white) and gumwater.

mezzotint An *intaglio* printmaking process in which the plate is ground all over with a *rocker*, leaving a burr raised on the surface that if inked would be rich black. The surface is subsequently lightened to a greater or lesser degree by scraping away the burr. The resulting *print* is also known as a *mezzotint.*

Minimalism A style of art, predominantly American, that dates from the mid-twentieth century, characterized by its rejection of expressive content and its use of "minimal" formal means.

modeling Changing from light to dark across the surface of an object to create a sense of volume and spatial illusions. In sculpture, the shaping of a form in some plastic material, such as clay or plaster; in drawing, painting, and printmaking, the rendering of a form, usually by means of *hatching* or *chiaroscuro*, to create the illusion of a three-dimensional form.

modernism The various strategies and directions employed in the twentieth century— *Cubism, Futurism, Expressionism,* etc.—to explore the particular formal properties of any given *medium.*

monochromatic color scheme A color composition consisting of one basic hue and closely related variants of it.

mosaic An art form in which small pieces of tile, glass, or stone are fitted together and embedded in cement on surfaces such as walls and floors.

narrative art A *temporal* form of art that tells a story.

naturalistic Synonymous with *representational;* descriptive of any work that resembles the natural world.

negative space Empty space, surrounding a positive shape and also the space between two positive shapes; sometimes referred to as interspace, field, void ground or empty space.

Neoclassicism A style of the late eighteenth and early nineteenth centuries that was influenced by the Greek *Classical style,* and that often employed Classical themes for its subject matter.

nonobjective art Art that makes no reference to the natural world and that explores the inherent expressive or aesthetic potential of the formal elements—line, shape, color—and the formal *compositional* principles of a given medium.

objective As opposed to *subjective,* free of personal feelings or emotion; hence, without bias.

one-point linear perspective A system for depicting *three-dimensional* depth on a *two-dimensional* surface, based upon the illusion that all parallel lines when receding into space will converge at a single point on the horizon, called the *vanishing point.* A version of *linear perspective* in which there is only one *vanishing point* in the *composition.*

Optical Painting (Op Art) An art style particularly popular in the 1960s in which line and color are manipulated in ways that stimulate the eye into believing it perceives movement.

optical or perceptual color The color as perceived by the eye, changed by the effects of light and atmosphere, in the way, for instance, that distant mountains appear to be blue.

organic shape A free-form, irregular shape. May also be known as *biomorphic* or *ameoboid* shape.

original print A *print* created by the artist alone and that has been printed by the artist or under the artist's direct supervision.

outline A line that can define only the outside edge of an object, not its contour, but a resulting silhouette of the form.

pastel (1) A soft crayon made of chalk and pigment. Also any work done in this *medium* . (2) A pale, light color.

pencil A drawing tool made of graphite encased in a soft wood cylinder.

perceptual line Any line that is perceived but not actually drawn, such as a horizon line.

performance art A form of art, popular especially since the late 1960s, that includes not only physical space but the human activity that goes on within it.

perspective A formula for projecting the illusion of *three-dimensional space* onto a *two-dimensional* surface. See also *linear perspective, one-point linear perspective, two-point linear perspective,* and *atmospheric perspective.*

photorealistic art Art rendered with such a high degree of *representational* accuracy that it appears to be photographed rather than drawn or painted.

picture plane The surface on which the artist works which is directly related to an imaginary piece of glass the size of the paper that could be placed between the artist and the subject. The picture plane contains the content of a work of art.

plane A two-dimensional, continuous surface with only one direction.

Pop Art A style arising in the early 1960s characterized by its emphasis on the forms and imagery of mass culture.

positive shape The actual shape of an actual object or form.

Post-Impressionism A name that describes the painting of a number of artists, working in widely different styles, in the last decades of the nineteenth century in France.

Postmodernism A term used to describe the willfully plural and eclectic art forms of contemporary art.

primary colors The hues that in theory cannot be created from a mixture of other hues and from which all other hues are created—namely, in pigment, red, yellow, and blue, and in light, red-orange, green, and blue-violet.

print Any one of multiple *impressions* made from a master image.

proof A trial *impression* of a *print*, made before the final *edition* is run, so that it may be examined and, if necessary, corrected.

proportion In any composition, the relationship between the parts and of the parts to the whole.

realism As opposed to *idealism,* the representation of things with relative fidelity to their appearance in visible nature.

relief (1) In sculpture, images and forms are attached to a background and project off it. See *low relief* and *high relief.* (2) In printmaking, any process in which any area of the plate not to be printed is carved away, leaving only the original surface to be printed.

representational art Any work of art that seeks to resemble the world of natural appearance.

reserve An area of a work of art that retains the original color and texture of the untouched surface or *ground.*

rocker A sharp, curved tool utilized in the *mezzotint* printmaking process.

Rococo A style of art popular in the first three-quarters of the eighteenth century, particularly in France, characterized by curvilinear forms, *pastel* colors, and its light, often frivolous subject matter.

Romanesque art The dominant style of art and architecture in Europe from the eighth to the twelfth centuries, characterized, in architecture, by Roman precedents, particularly the round *arch* and the *barrel vault.*

Romanticism A dramatic, emotional, and *subjective* art arising in the early nineteenth century in opposition to the austere discipline of *Neoclassicism.*

scale The comparative size of a thing in relation to another like thing, or its "normal" or "expected" size.

scribbled-line gesture A type of drawing that uses a tight, overlapping network of tangled lines to create the volume of a figure or object without drawing an outline.

secondary colors A *hue* created by combining two *primary colors*; in pigment, the secondary colors are traditionally considered to be orange, green, and blue; in light, yellow, magenta, and cyan.

shade A color or *hue* modified by the addition of another color resulting in a hue of lower *key* or *value,* in the way, for instance, that the addition of black to red results in maroon.

sighting A visual measurement of objects and the spaces bewteen objects.

simulated texture The imitation of the tactile quality of a surface; ranging from a highly illusionistic duplication to a suggested imitation of the subject's texture.

simultaneous contrast A property of *complementary colors* when placed side by side, resulting in the fact that both appear brighter and more intense than when seen in isolation.

spectrum The colored bands of visible light created when sunlight passes through a prism.

still life A work of art that consists of an arrangement of inanimate objects, such as flowers, fruit, and household objects.

stippling In drawing and printmaking, a pattern of closely placed dots or small marks employed to create the effect of shading or *modeling*.

stump A rolled paper tool used to blend pastels and charcoal. The stump lends itself to soft build ups of value without marks. Stumps should be made out of rag paper rolled tightly with a pointed tip.

style Any constant, recurring, or conventional manner of treatment or execution of works of art that is characteristic of a particular civilization, time period, artistic movement, or individual artist.

subject matter The literal, visible image in a work of art, as distinguished from its *content*, which includes the connotative, symbolic, and suggestive aspects of the image.

subjective As opposed to *objective*, full of personal emotions and feelings.

sublime That which impresses the mind with a sense of grandeur and power, inspiring a sense of awe.

subtractive (1) In color, the adjective used to describe the fact that, when different *hues* of colored pigment are combined, the resulting mixture is lower in *key* than the original hues and duller as well, and as more and more hues are added, the resulting mixture is closer and closer to black.

Super realism See *photorealistic art.*

Surrealism A style of art of the early twentieth century that emphasized dream imagery, chance operations, and rapid, thoughtless forms of notation that expressed, it was felt, the unconscious mind.

symbol An image, sign, or element, such as a color, that is understood, by *convention* or context, to suggest some other meaning.

symmetry When two halves of a *composition* correspond to one another in terms of size, shape, and placement of forms.

texture The actual tactile characteristics of a thing, or the visual simulation of such characteristics.

three-dimensional space   Any space that possesses height, width, and depth.

tint   A color or *hue* modified by the addition of another color, resulting in a hue of higher *key* or *value*, in the way, for instance, that the addition of white to red results in pink.

trompe l'oeil   A form of representation that attempts to depict the object as if it were actually present before the eye in *three-dimensional space;* literally "eye-fooling."

two-dimensional space   Any space that is flat, possessing height and width, but no depth, such as a piece of drawing paper or a canvas.

two-point linear perspective   A version of *linear perspective* in which there are two (or more) *vanishing points* in the *composition.*

value   The gradation of tone from light to dark, from white through gray to black. The relative darkness or lightness of a color.

value scale   The range from white through gray to black in gradual gradated units. The human eye is probably capable of seeing a range of ten changes.

vanishing point   In *linear perspective,* the point on the horizon line where parallel lines appear to converge.

video art   An art form that employs television as its *medium.*

virtual reality   An artificial three-dimensional *environment,* generated through the use of computers, that the viewer experiences as real space.

volume   Form that has height, width, and depth.

watercolor   A painting *medium* consisting of pigments suspended in a solution of water and gum arabic.